Rope

Patrick Hamilton

A SAMUEL FRENCH ACTING EDITION

FOUNDED 1830

SAMUELFRENCH.COM
SAMUELFRENCH-LONDON.CO.UK

FOR PRODUCTION ENQUIRIES

UNITED STATES AND CANADA
Info@SamuelFrench.com
1-866-598-8449

UNITED KINGDOM AND EUROPE
Theatre@SamuelFrench-London.co.uk
020-7255-4302

Each title is subject to availability from Samuel French, depending upon country of performance. Please be aware that ROPE may not be licensed by Samuel French in your territory. Professional and amateur producers should contact the nearest Samuel French office or licensing partner to verify availability.

MUSIC USE NOTE

Licensees are solely responsible for obtaining formal written permission from copyright owners to use copyrighted music in the performance of this play and are strongly cautioned to do so. If no such permission is obtained by the licensee, then the licensee must use only original music that the licensee owns and controls. Licensees are solely responsible and liable for all music clearances and shall indemnify the copyright owners of the play(s) and their licensing agent, Samuel French, against any costs, expenses, losses and liabilities arising from the use of music by licensees. Please contact the appropriate music licensing authority in your territory for the rights to any incidental music.

IMPORTANT BILLING AND CREDIT REQUIREMENTS

If you have obtained performance rights to this title, please refer to your licensing agreement for important billing and credit requirements.

ROPE

First presented by The Repertory Players at the Strand
Theatre, London, on 3rd March, 1929, with the following
cast:

Wyndham Brandon	Sebastian Shaw
Charles Granillo	Anthony Ireland
Sabot	Frederick Burtwell
Kenneth Raglan	Hugh Dempster
Leila Arden	Betty Schuster
Sir Johnstone Kentley	Daniel Roe
Mrs Debenham	Ruth Taylor
Rupert Cadell	Robert Holmes

The first London West End production was by Reginald
Denham at the Ambassadors' Theatre, London, on
25th April, 1929, with the following cast:

Wyndham Brandon	Brian Aherne
Charles Granillo	Anthony Ireland
Sabot	Stafford Hilliard
Kenneth Raglan	Patrick Waddington
Leila Arden	Lilian Oldland
Sir Johnstone Kentley	Paul Gill
Mrs Debenham	Alix Frizell
Rupert Cadell	Ernest Milton

ROPE

Presented at the Almeida Theatre, London, on 10th December, 2009, with the following cast and creative team:

Wyndham Brandon	Blake Ritson
Charles Granillo	Alex Waldmann
Sabot	Philip Arditti
Kenneth Raglan	Henry Lloyd-Hughes
Leila Arden	Phoebe Waller-Bridge
Sir Johnstone Kentley	Michael Elwyn
Mrs Debenham	Emma Dewhurst
Rupert Cadell	Bertie Carvel

Directed by Roger Michell
Designed by Mark Thompson
Lighting by Rick Fisher
Sound design by John Leonard

CHARACTERS

Wyndham Brandon, young
Charles Granillo, a Spaniard, young
Kenneth Raglan, very young
Leila Arden, young
Sir Johnstone Kentley, old
Mrs Debenham, about fifty
Rupert Cadell, about twenty-nine

The action of the play takes place in a room on the first floor of the house in Mayfair, London, shared by Brandon and Granillo

Time — 1929

To
Reginald Denham

ACT I

A room on the first floor of the house in Mayfair shared by Brandon and Granillo. Eight-forty p.m.

The room is a combination of a study and a drawing-room. At the back, R, there are long french windows. There is a door L, next to a fireplace, which has a mirror above it and books and a box of cigarettes on the mantelpiece

The room is furnished in a luxurious and faintly bizarre manner and on no discernible model. Nevertheless, there are really many good things about if you care to look for them. To the L of the french windows is a fine grandfather clock. Next L, against the wall, is a wireless set. Next, a large divan. DL are an armchair and a small table with an ashtray on it. In the UR corner is a baby grand piano, with stool. Against the R wall is a sideboard with glasses and drinks on it, and a pair of silver nutcrackers. There is a table DR with a lamp and a book on it; to the L of this table is an armchair. DC is a large chest. There is a telephone

The heavy curtains at the french windows, and all the room's upholstery, are red

The CURTAIN *rises. The clock stands at eight-forty at night. (NB: The action of the play is continuous, and the fall of the curtain at the end of each act denotes the lapse of no time whatever) The red curtains are open and there is a fire burning in the grate, but this is not discernible at first. The room is completely darkened save for the pallid gleam from lamplight in the street below, which comes through the window. Against this are silhouetted the figures of Granillo and Brandon*

Brandon is tall, finely athletically built, and blond. He is quietly and expensively dressed, with a double-breasted waistcoat, which shows his sturdiness off to the best advantage, and perfectly creased trousers, not turned up at the end, and about nineteen inches in width. His hands are large, and his build is that of the boxer — not the football player or the runner. He has clever blue eyes, a fine mouth and nose, and a rich, competent and really easy voice. He is plainly very well-off, and seems to have used his money in making a fine specimen of himself instead of running to seed. He is almost paternal with everyone he addresses, and this seems to arise from an instinctive knowledge of his own good health, good looks, success and natural calm, as opposed to the harassed frailty of the ordinary human being. This, however, brings him at moments to an air of vague priggishness and self-approbation, and is the one reason why you cannot altogether like him

Granillo is slim, not so tall as Brandon, expensively and rather ornately dressed in a dark blue suit with four-pocket waistcoat. He wears a diamond ring. He is dark. A Spaniard. He is enormously courteous — something between dancing-master and stage villain. He speaks English perfectly. To those who know him fairly well, and are not subject to Anglo-Saxon prejudices, he seems a thoroughly good sort

Brandon and Granillo are bending over the chest, intent, working at something — exactly what, we cannot discern. The silence is complete. Suddenly the lid of the chest falls with a bang

Brandon goes over to the window and closes the heavy curtains; the room is now in complete black-out. They continue whatever they are doing

Brandon (*murmuring*) All right, all right.

Pause. Brandon moves DR and switches on the lamp at the little table

Granillo (*by the chest*) Put out that light! Put out that light!

Brandon switches the light out

Brandon Steady, Granno. (*He sits in the DR armchair and lights a cigarette with a match*)

The cigarette glows in the darkness. Pause

Feeling yourself, Granno?

No answer

Feeling yourself again, Granno?

No answer

Granno.
Granillo Give me some matches.
Brandon Matches? Here you are. Coming. (*He throws the matches over*)

The matches can be heard rattling in the air and falling on the floor. Granillo picks them up and lights his own cigarette. The two pin-points of light are all that come from the darkness. Pause

It's about time you pulled yourself together, isn't it, Granno? Sabot will be here in a quarter of an hour.

Pause

Granillo You fully understand, Brandon, what we've done?
Brandon Do I know what I've done? ... Yes. I know quite well what I've done. (*His voice becomes rich, easy, powerful, elated and yet withal slightly defiant*) I have done murder.
Granillo Yes.
Brandon (*continuing in the same voice*) I have committed murder. I have committed passionless — motiveless — faultless — and clueless murder. Bloodless and noiseless murder.
Granillo Yes.
Brandon And immaculate murder. I have killed. I have killed for sake of danger and for the sake of killing. And I am alive. Truly and wonderfully alive. That is what I have done, Granno.

Long pause

What's the matter? Are you getting superstitious?
Granillo No. I'm not superstitious.
Brandon (*suavely*) Then may I put on the light?
Granillo No. You mayn't ...

The fire glows faintly; the figures of Brandon and Granillo may now be dimly discerned

During the following Granillo moves DS and sits in the armchair L

Brandon?
Brandon Yes?
Granillo You remember when Ronald came in?
Brandon What do you mean — "when Ronald came in"?
Granillo When Ronald came in here — when he came in from the car. You were standing at the door.
Brandon Yes.
Granillo Did you see anyone standing there? Up the street -- about seventy yards?

Brandon Well, what of it?

Granillo Oh, nothing … Brandon …

Brandon Yes?

Granillo When I met Ronald. When I met him — coming out of the Coliseum … When I met him, and got him into the car — why shouldn't someone have seen us?

Brandon What do you mean by someone?

Granillo Oh, someone. Anyone. Did we think of that, Brandon?

Brandon I *did*.

Pause

Granillo It's in the room, you know. Do you think we'll get away with it?

Brandon When? Tonight?

Granillo Yes.

Brandon Are you suggesting that some psychic force, emanating from that chest there, is going to advise Sir Johnstone Kentley of the fact that the remains — or shall I say the lifeless entirety — of his twenty-year-old son and heir is contained therein? (*Pause*) My dear Granillo, if you are feeling in any way insecure, perhaps I had better fortify you with a brief summary of facts — with mathematics, as it were. Let me please give you — —

Granillo Listen!

There is a tense stillness

Brandon What *are* … ?

Granillo Listen, I tell you!

There is another pause. Granillo springs up, goes over to the window, and peeps through the curtains

It's all right. I thought it was Sabot. (*He sits in the* L *chair again*)

Brandon Sabot, in the first place, will not be here until five minutes to nine, if then, for Sabot is seldom punctual. Sabot, in the second place, has been deprived by a wily master of his key. He will therefore ring. Let me, I say, give you a cool narration of our transactions. This afternoon, at about two o'clock, young Ronald Kentley, our fellow-undergraduate, left his father's house with the object of visiting the Coliseum Music Hall. He did so. After the performance he was met in the street by your good self, and invited to this house. He was then given tea, and at six forty-five precisely, done to death by strangulation and rope. He was subsequently deposited in that chest. Tonight, at nine o'clock, his father, Sir Johnstone Kentley, his aunt, Mrs Debenham, and three well-chosen friends of our own will come round here for regalement. They will talk small talk and depart. After the party, at eleven o'clock — —

Granillo (*interrupting*) This party isn't a slip, is it, Brandon?

Brandon My dear Granno, have we not already agreed that the entire beauty and piquancy of the evening will reside in the party itself? (*Pause*) At eleven o' clock tonight, I was saying, you and I will leave by car for Oxford. We will carry our fellow-undergraduate. Our fellow-undergraduate will never be heard of again. Our fellow-undergraduate will not be murdered. He will be missing. That is the complete story, and the perfection of criminality — the complete story of the perfect crime. (*Pause*) I am quite lucid — am I not?

Granillo Yes.

Brandon The party itself, you see, Granno, so far from being our vulnerable point, is the very apex, as it were, and consummation of our feat. Consider its ingredients. I still don't think we could have chosen better. There will be, first, and by all means foremost, Sir Johnstone Kentley — the father of the — occupant of the chest. It is he, as the father, who gives the entire *macabre* quality of the evening. Well chosen, so far. We then, of course, require his wife; but she, being an invalid, is unobtainable, and we have procured, instead his sister. The same thing applies to her.

The telephone rings. Granillo springs up and goes over to it in the darkness

Granillo (*into the telephone*) Hallo. … Hallo. … Hallo. What? This is Mayfair X143. … What? What? Hallo.

Brandon turns on the lamp

Put out that light! Put out that light, I tell you!

Brandon promptly switches the lamp off

Brandon Steady, Granno.

Granillo (*into the telephone*) Hallo. … Hallo. …

Brandon Will you put down that receiver, Granno? You're telling London you're afraid. (*Pause*) Come and sit down.

Granillo puts down the receiver, goes over to the window and peers out again. He then moves to the door and opens it

Granillo creeps out into passage and closes the door behind him

Suddenly a click is heard. A light comes on in the passage beyond the door; light filters in round the door. Brandon remains motionless. The light goes out again

Granillo enters the room, shutting the door. He takes his seat again

There is a slight pause

Granillo Well, go on.

Brandon There are then Kenneth Raglan and Leila Arden. They have been asked for their youth, innocence, and good spirits alone. Also, in Raglan, who went to the same school and is at the same university as ourselves, you have about the most perfect specimen of ordinary humanity obtainable, and therefore a suitable witness to this so extraordinary scene. Unintellectual humanity is represented. The same applies to Leila, his female counterpart … We then come to Rupert … Now in Rupert, Granno, we have a very intriguing proposition. Rupert, in fact, is about the one man alive who might have seen this thing from our angle, that is, the artistic one. You will recall that we even contemplated, at one time, inviting him to share our dangers, and we eventually turned the notion down, not necessarily because it would have been too much for him to swallow intellectually, but simply because he would not have had the nerve. Rupert is a damnably brilliant poet, but perhaps a little too fastidious … He could have invented and admired, but he could not have acted. So he is in the same blissless ignorance as the rest. Nevertheless he is intellect's representative, and valued at that. (*Pause*) Granno …

No answer

   Granno.

Granillo Yes.

Brandon What's the time?

Granillo lights a match and holds it up to the clock

Granillo Ten to.

Brandon Sabot will be here in five minutes.

Granillo I know.

Brandon May I put on the light?

Granillo Must you? Can't you go on talking?

Brandon No, I can't, I'm afraid.

Granillo (*after a pause*) Go on. I'm all right. Put it on. I'm better now.

Brandon switches on the lamp. He looks into the light of the lamp, employing himself by fiddling with the shade

Granillo walks over to the mirror over the mantelpiece, looks at himself and adjusts his collar. He takes a cigarette from the box on the mantelpiece, strikes a match and lights it. Simultaneously, Brandon rises and moves to the mantelpiece. He takes a cigarette just in time to have it lit from Granillo's match. He puts his arm round Granillo and does this

Brandon (*puffing on the cigarette*) Thank you. I thought you were going to lose your nerve for a moment, Granno.
Granillo So did I. But I wasn't.
Brandon May I put on the light proper?
Granillo Yes.

Brandon, humming with a rather strained nonchalance, moves to the switch by the door and turns on the overhead light

Brandon exits without a word, closing the door

The passage light comes on with a click

Granillo remains looking into the fire for about thirty seconds, then goes over to the sideboard and takes a drink

Brandon enters suddenly. His eyes are blazing, and he is pale with rage. He is holding a slip of blue paper

Brandon God, you fool! Didn't I tell you to check up in there!
Granillo What?
Brandon (*holding the slip of blue paper in front of Granillo*) Look at this! The boy's Coliseum ticket. It was on the floor. We could hang on that! What in heaven's name … ?
Granillo (*with a shrug of the shoulders characteristic of his race*) But, my dear Brandon, you are as much to blame as myself.
Brandon That's nothing to do with it! It's your business to see what I don't see. How in heaven's name it got there I don't know.

The doorbell rings

Damnation! That's Sabot. Now for God's sake quiet yourself and sit down. All right. I'll go.

Brandon gives Granillo the ticket and exits

Granillo slips the blue ticket into his top waistcoat pocket, rushes over and finishes his drink, seizes the book from the table, and settles down in the R armchair, pretending to read

Pause

The voices of Brandon and Sabot come from outside, as if they are mounting stairs. They arrive outside the door

Sabot (*off*) In here, sair?
Brandon (*off*) Yes, in here.
Sabot (*off*) Very good, sair.

Brandon enters, closing the door behind him. He settles down in the L *armchair*

There is a knock upon the door. Brandon rises quickly and opens it

Sabot, in an overcoat, is at the door, with a newspaper in his hand. He is an alert, very dark little Frenchman, with a long nose and a blueness of cheek which no amount of shaving will eradicate. He is an almost perfect servant — intelligent, alert and obedient, but not, perhaps, completely impersonal — his employers being in the habit of making the occasional advances towards him. Whoever he is with, he has an air of being breathlessly anxious to apologize for something or anything. He is married, quietly ambitious, industrious, and will have a restaurant of his own one of these days

Sabot Ze evening paper, sair?
Brandon (*taking the newspaper*) Oh — thank you very much, Sabot.
Sabot I thought you might like to look at it, sair. (*He smiles shyly*)
Brandon Very welcome, Sabot. Many thanks.
Sabot Not at all, sair.

Brandon closes the door in Sabot's face

Brandon comes down to the armchair L. *Granillo watches him. Brandon catches Granillo's eye but looks away again. He opens the paper*

Brandon (*his eyes fixed on the paper*) Sorry for my little outburst, Granno. But it rather upset me.
Granillo (*his eyes fixed on the book*) Not at all. You're quite correct. I should have seen it. How it got there I don't know.
Brandon Neither do I. What's the time?
Granillo (*comparing his wrist-watch with the clock*) About five to.
Brandon We can expect our first guest.
Granillo Yes.

Sabot enters, carrying a large tray with table linen, cutlery, plates, sandwiches et cetera on it. He deposits it on the sideboard, then moves C *and looks first at Granillo and then at Brandon. He addresses Brandon*

Sabot Ze table, sair?

Brandon (*his eyes on the paper*) Yes. That's all right. (*Indicating the chest*) Lay it there, will you? We're using the table for books.

Sabot But I can bring ze table from upstairs, sair?

Brandon Oh, no. That's all right, Sabot. Lay it there.

Sabot No, sair, it will be no trouble to bring from upstairs.

Brandon (*suavely*) Nevertheless, Sabot, lay it there, will you?

Sabot (*a little shamefaced at this snub; under his breath*) Very good, sair. (*He moves to the sideboard. During the following he lays the tablecloth and other items on the chest*)

There is a long pause

Brandon (*referring to the paper*) Hallo — Hammond at it again. (*He turns the paper over and finds the "Stop Press"*) 106 not ... How many's that, Sabot?

Sabot The tenth, sair. (*Pause*) He was missed at twenty-one, sair.

Brandon (*again referring to the paper*) I'm getting rather tired of "Inquests on London Girls" ... Also of "Plucky London Typists' Brave Attempts" ... Also of Jim and Amy ...

The doorbell rings

Ah — here we are. He's early, whoever he is.

Sabot To bring in here, sair?

Brandon Yes — in here.

Sabot exits

Granillo rises, goes over to the piano, and commences to play "Dance Little Lady" with a rather unpleasant brilliance. He looks significantly at Brandon while playing. He finishes the tune, leaves off, and takes a drink at the sideboard. He now looks quite at ease and pleased with himself

Sabot enters and holds the door open. Kenneth Raglan enters

Raglan is very young, fair, simple, good-looking, shy, foolish and good. He has no ideas whatever. He still thinks that nightclubs are dens of delight, but that there is probably one girl in the world for him whom he will one day find. His pathetic ideal, in his bearing before the world, is sophistication. To hear him alluding to a "simply staggering binge, old boy," when he has merely got mildly intoxicated, is to have exemplified at once his sense of humour and wickedness. In the presence of Granillo and Brandon he is merely, of course, tentative and hopeless. He is in evening dress

Sabot exits

Raglan (*coming forward nervously*) Hallo.
Brandon (*taking Raglan's hand cordially*) Hallo, Raglan, old man. Come right in. You know Granillo, don't you?

Granillo comes forward cordially

Raglan Rather.

Raglan and Granillo shake hands

Granillo Quite a long time since we met, though. (*He smiles*)
Raglan Yes — isn't it? (*He looks round nervously*) I say, I'm terribly sorry. I've come dressed.
Brandon My dear fellow, my fault entirely. Come and seat yourself.

Brandon affectionately leads Raglan to a chair

I should have explained. You know we're going up to Oxford tonight?
Raglan Oh, no — are you? I'm not going up till Friday.
Brandon Now what are you going to drink? You can have gin and Italian … Or gin and Angostura. And I can do you a very nice gin and French.
Raglan I should like gin and It, I think.
Brandon Gin and It? Right. (*He goes over to the sideboard, opens the bottles and pours the drink carefully during the following*) Yes, we leave tonight about twelve, and travel by (*he pours*) automobile — in the (*he pours more*) let us hope — moonlight. And of course all this place is simply covered (*he pours more*) with books.
Raglan Covered with books?
Brandon (*giving Raglan his drink*) Yes. I've come into a library.
Raglan Come into a library?
Brandon (*going to the sideboard to pour a drink for himself*) Of course, books aren't really in your line, are they, Kenneth? (*He opens a fresh bottle*)
Raglan No — not really. Only P. G. Wodehouse.
Granillo Oh — are you good at P. G. Wodehouse?
Raglan Yes. Why? Are you?
Granillo Yes — rather.
Raglan Good Lord — I shouldn't have thought you would have been.
Granillo Oh, rather …
Brandon (*pouring his drink*) Did you ever hear of old Gerry Wickham, Kenneth? An uncle of mine.

Raglan Oh, yes — rather.

Brandon Well, you know he's died just lately.

Raglan Oh — has he? Yes?

Brandon Well, it's *his* library (*he pours*) which he has very kindly (*he pours*) *and* unexpectedly (*he pours*) bestowed upon me.

Raglan Good Lord!

Brandon To the unspeakable mortification of Sir Johnstone Kentley.

Raglan Oh, Sir Johnstone Kentley. He's quite a famous collector, isn't he?

Brandon Yes. He's coming here to-night.

Raglan Good heavens — is he? It *is* the same man, isn': it? He lives in Grosvenor Square and has a son.

Brandon (*after a pause*) Quite right, Kenneth. He lives in Grosvenor Square (*he pauses*) and has a son. (*He moves* DS *with his own drink, lights a cigarette, and sits down*) He also runs to a sister, and she's coming too.

Raglan Oh — really?

Brandon Yes. A reward of ten pounds is offered to any person or persons forcing, by dynamite or other means, more than two words out of her at the same time.

Raglan Why — is she uncommunicative?

Brandon "Is she uncommunicative? … " Uncommunicative, Kenneth, is not the word.

Raglan Really? Tell me, Sir Johnstone's son. Isn't that Ronald Kentley, the lad who's so frightfully good at sports?

Brandon That's right. You don't know him, do you?

Raglan No. I've never met him, but he wins hurdles, and hundreds of yards, and things like that, doesn't he?

Brandon Yes. That's right. As a matter of fact, he's the living image of yourself. Isn't he, Granno?

Granillo Yes. He is like.

Raglan Me? In what way?

Brandon Oh, in every way. Same age. Same height. Same colour. Same sweet and refreshing innocence.

Raglan Oh, shut up. I'm not an athlete, anyway.

Brandon No. But you're just as much alive. In fact more so.

Raglan (*awkwardly*) Am I? Then you're having Sir Johnstone here just sort of to make him grind his teeth with envy about the books, then?

Brandon On the contrary, I'm going to let him have exactly what he wants — provided I don't want it. But I'm telling you all this, Kenneth, just to excuse the terrible mess we're in. You'll observe that we're having a meal off a chest.

Raglan Oh, yes. (*He looks at the chest*) I thought it looked rather weird.

Brandon Good Lord, Kenneth. You're getting positively fat.

Raglan Am I?

Brandon Nothing like the little boy who used to fag for me at school.
Raglan Lord! That's a long while ago.
Brandon Oh, it doesn't seem so very long.
Raglan Of course, I used to think you an absolute hero in those days, Brandon.
Brandon Did you? Well, as a matter of fact, I was always more or less popular amongst the juniors.
Granillo It was I who was the unpopular one.
Brandon Were you unpopular, Granno?
Raglan Oh, yes, I remember I used to loathe you in those days.
Granillo There you are.
Brandon Why did you loathe him?
Raglan Oh, I don't know. I suppose games were the only things that ever counted in those days. I'm sure it was most unreasonable.
Granillo It was, I assure you. I'm very harmless.

The doorbell rings

Brandon Here we are. I wonder if that's Rupert. Did you ever meet Rupert, Kenneth? Rupert Cadell?
Raglan No — I can't say I have.
Brandon No — he was before your time, wasn't he? (*He rises, goes to the door, and opens it*) Ah-ha, the ravishing Leila! Come along, my dear, this way.

Leila Arden enters. She, like Raglan, is young, good-looking, and has no ideas. She also has the same tendency to conceal that deficiency with a show of sophistication. In this she is perhaps more successful than Raglan. She has a fairly good stock of many-syllabled and rather outré words which she brings out with a rather comic emphasis, rolling her eyes the while, as though she doesn't really mean what she is saying. In this way she never actually commits herself to any emotion or feeling, and might even be thought deep. But she is not

Brandon How are you, Leila? You know Granno, don't you?
Leila Hallo.

Leila and Granillo shake hands

Brandon And this is Kenneth. Mr Raglan — Miss Arden.
Leila Hallo.
Raglan Hallo.

Leila and Raglan shake hands. Brandon indicates a chair between Raglan and Granillo and Leila sits down

Brandon Now what are you going to have, Leila? Kenneth's having a gin and It.
Leila I'd adore one.

Brandon goes to the sideboard and mixes Leila's drink. There is a rather awkward silence

(*To Granillo*) And how are *you* getting on?
Granillo Very well, thanks. And how are you?
Leila Oh, I'm all right. (*She turns and grins at Raglan*)

Raglan is only too willing to grin at Leila

Of course, I simply *know* — that I've seen you somewhere before.
Raglan (*looking foolish*) Really?
Leila You're not a Frinton-on-Sea expert, are you?
Raglan No. I just go there occasionally, that's all.
Leila How weird! Because I could simply *swear* that I've seen you somewhere before.
Raglan (*grinning*) Oh — how weird!
Brandon (*giving Leila her drink*) Previous incarnation, I expect. Here you are, Leila. Excuse mess. We're in a horrible mess here altogether. Kenneth'll tell you about it. I've come into a library.
Leila Come into a library, my dear? My dear, how weird!
Brandon Yes. And I hope you don't think you're going to get anything to eat, because all the servants are away and we're very humble.
Leila No — you told me that, and I had a simply *gluttonous* high tea. *Gorged*, my dear!
Brandon Oh, well, that's all right. I really wouldn't have asked you — only this is the last chance of seeing you before we go.
Leila Are you going up tonight, then?
Brandon Yes.
Raglan Of course, I'm feeling absolutely ghastly — coming dressed like this.
Leila Why? I'm sure I ought to be dressed too. (*She turns to Brandon*) Of course you must admit, my dear, this is a most mysterious and weird meal.
Granillo (*a little too heavily*) Why mysterious and weird?

Leila senses Granillo's heaviness; this causes a faintly embarrassed little pause

Oh — I don't know. Just mysterious. And weird. (*Pause. To Raglan*) Don't *you* think it's mysterious and weird? Such a queer time, to begin with.

The doorbell rings

Brandon (*cutting in rather loudly*) Here we are. I'll bet you that's old Kentley. Forgive me a moment. I must go and usher him in.

Brandon exits, leaving the door open

Voices can be heard from below

Leila (*softly, rolling her eyes*) Who's the newcomer?
Granillo (*rising and putting his cigarette out in the ashtray on the table*)The newcomer, Leila, is the revered Sir Johnstone Kentley, who has come here to look at books.
Leila My dear!
Granillo Unless it's Rupert — which it may be, of course. (*He moves to the door*)

Brandon, Sir Johnstone Kentley, and Mrs Debenham enter

Raglan stands

During the following, Sabot comes in after Kentley et al., and quietly goes on with the laying of plates, knives, sandwiches et cetera on the chest

Sir Johnstone is a decidedly pleasant old gentleman, slightly bent, old for his years, with clear grey eyes — slow-moving, utterly harmless, gentle and a little listless. His listlessness and gentleness, however, derive not alone from a natural kindliness, but also from the fact that he has been in a position of total authority throughout the greater part of his life, and has had no need to assert himself. But he has only too plainly never abused that authority, and the whole effect of him is completely captivating

Mrs Debenham is the sister of Sir Johnstone. She is tallish, plainly dressed, has been widowed long, is very plain, about fifty. She hardly ever opens her mouth, her sole means of expression being a sudden, broad, affable smirk. This she switches on, in a terrifying way, every now and again, but immediately relapses into the lost, miserable, absent-minded gloom which characterizes her. She is, indeed, so completely a nonentity as to acquire considerable personality and distinction from the very fact

Sir Johnstone (*talking as he enters*) ... which of course, can never be done. Ah, how do you do, Granillo. How are you getting on?

Sir Johnstone and Granillo shake hands

You know my sister, don't you?
Mrs Debenham Yes! (*She smirks*)

Mrs Debenham and Granillo shake hands

Raglan looks sheepish and Leila does not quite know what to do with herself

Brandon (*taking the stage*) Now let me introduce you all ... This, Mrs Debenham, is Miss Leila Arden ... Miss Arden — Sir Johnstone Kentley.

Leila and Sir Johnstone shake hands

Leila Howdyoudo.
Sir Johnstone Howdyoudo.
Brandon And this is Mr Kenneth Raglan.

Raglan and Sir Johnstone shake hands

Raglan Howdyoudo, sir.
Sir Johnstone Howdyoudo.

Mrs Debenham smirks

There is an embarrassed pause

Brandon And there we are. And here, Sir Johnstone, is an armchair which I think is more or less in your line.

Brandon leads Sir Johnstone down to a chair; Sir Johnstone sits

And here is a chest, from which we're going to feed, the table having been commandeered for books.

During the following, Granillo makes sure that everyone is seated again and moves to stand at the mantelpiece

Sir Johnstone (*peering at the chest*) That's not a Cassone, is it?

Brandon No, sir. It's not genuine, it's a reproduction. But it's a rather nice piece. I got it in Italy. (*To Sir Johnstone*) Now will you have a cocktail, sir?

Sir Johnstone Good heavens, no, my boy. (*He looks vaguely about the room*)

Brandon And you, Mrs Debenham?

Mrs Debenham merely smirks

You *won't?*

Mrs Debenham Oh, yes, please.

Brandon Ah. Good. Now what will you have? Will you have a gin and Angostura, or a gin and French, or a gin and Italian?

Mrs Debenham Yes, please. (*During the following her mind drifts off elsewhere so she is not paying attention*)

Sir Johnstone These books I'm going to see — where are they, Brandon?

Brandon (*going to the sideboard again and mixing Mrs Debenham's drink*) Oh, the books. They're in the other room. The dining-room. I laid them out as well as I could, and there's more space in there.

Sir Johnstone I shall be interested to see them — most interested … I seem to remember that Wickham had a really remarkable little lot of Shakespeariana …

Brandon Yes. But I'm afraid the Folios were sold before he died. But there's a run of the Quartos, and a really amazing lot of Baconian stuff. At least, I'm told it's very fine.

The doorbell rings

Sabot exits quickly

Sir Johnstone Ah-ha. Bacon, my boy. That's a special favourite of mine.

Leila Of course, all this is *too* technical and peculiar!

Raglan Yes — isn't it?

Brandon I expect Mrs Debenham has learnt to put up with this sort of thing, hasn't she?

There is a pause. Mrs Debenham snaps to attention and suddenly realizes she is being addressed

Mrs Debenham Oh, yes!

Leila Of course, I'm *too* philistine for words. Do go on. What about Bacon?

Sir Johnstone I think we'd better try and restrain ourselves, my boy.

Leila Oh no. Do go on. You must tell us about Bacon. Isn't he the the person who dashes round *being* Shakespeare, or something like that?

Rupert Cadell enters and stands in the doorway. He is of medium height and about twenty-nine. He is a little foppish in dress and appearance, and this impression is increased by the very exquisite walking-stick which he carries indoors as well as out. He is lame in the right leg. He is enormously affected in speech and carriage. He brings his words out not only as though he is infinitely weary of all things, but also as though articulation is causing him some definite physical pain which he is trying to circumvent by keeping his head and body perfectly still. His sentences are often involved, but nearly always syntactically complete. His affectation almost verges on effeminacy, and can be very irritating, but he has a very disarming habit, every now and again, of retrieving the whole thing with an extraordinary frank, open and genial smile

Brandon Ah, here he is, here he is! The last, as usual. Come along in, Rupert.

Rupert moves a little into the room

Brandon introduces Rupert to the others. Rupert smiles at each of them

Mr Cadell — Mrs Debenham.

Mrs Debenham smirks

Rupert Howdyoudo.
Brandon Miss Leila Arden.
Rupert Howdyoudo.
Leila Howdyoudo.
Brandon Mr Cadell — Sir Johnstone Kentley.
Rupert (*a little more solemnly, no smile on his face*) Howdyoudo, sir.
Sir Johnstone Howdyoudo.
Brandon Mr Raglan — Mr Cadell.
Raglan Howdyoudo.

Rupert bows

Rupert But tell me. I don't quite follow. Have I come dressed, or have others come undressed? I telephoned an inquiry, but could not obtain — er — any answer.
Brandon Now contain yourself, Rupert, and sit down. (*He indicates a chair*)

Rupert looks at the chair, then espies the chest. He stops affectedly, bends down to look at the chest and prods it with his stick. He pauses

Rupert What in heaven … ?

Brandon There you are, Rupert, we're going to have our meal off a chest.

Rupert Oh — are we?

Brandon Yes.

Rupert (*prodding the chest*) Why are we going to have our meal off a chest?

Brandon Because it's a very nice chest, and because all the tables are covered with books.

Leila Yes. Haven't you heard? The entire place is covered with library.

Rupert Oh! (*He looks round, limps to a chair and sits down*)

Brandon Now, Rupert, are you going to have a cocktail?

Rupert No. Thank you. I have had four already.

Raglan ⎫ (*together*) Four!
Leila ⎭

Rupert Yes. Why? Aren't I carrying my drink?

Leila Oh, yes — you're carrying it all right. It's just rather a mean advantage, that's all.

Brandon (*to Sabot*) That's all right, Sabot. I'll ring when we're through. Then you can clear and get away.

Sabot Thank you, sair.

Sabot exits

Rupert When do we begin to have our meal off a chest? Because I'm personally rather peckish.

Brandon We're starting right away, Rupert. (*He moves to the chest*) Now look here, you people, there are a lot of plates and knives and things here — and lots of sandwiches and things — pâté, caviare, and salmon and cucumber, and what-not ... All you've got to do is to rally round and gather what you want ...

They all rise and gather garrulously around the chest, offering each other different dishes, et cetera. Eventually, and still talking, they resume their places. Sir Johnstone and Rupert now have glasses of wine; Leila has champagne

Mrs Debenham drifts off into inattention during the following

Sir Johnstone (*to Rupert*) Are you the great Cadell, then?

Leila, having her first gulp at her champagne, gives a long, satisfied sigh, "Ahhhhhhh!" Rupert stops to look at her, in his own fashion, and then looks at Sir Johnstone again

Rupert Why, do you know anything about me?

Sir Johnstone Oh — I've read your poems — that's all. Or at least a lot of them.

Rupert Dear me. I hope you're not confusing me with the other Caddell, sir.
Sir Johnstone No. I don't think so. You write poems, don't you?
Rupert I am told so, sir. But then so does the other Caddell. A devastating creature who spells it with two ds.
Sir Johnstone Oh, no. There's no confusion.
Granillo I never knew you could spell Cadell with two ds.
Leila Same here.
Raglan Yes, same here. I knew a Cadell once, and she used to spell it with only one d. Louisa Cadell. Horrible old hag she was, too. She lived in Bayswater.
Rupert Dear heaven. The young man is alluding to my aunt.
Raglan Oh, I say. I'm terribly sorry. Have I dropped a brick?
Rupert No. You have said a mouthful. (*He gets up*) Can I have another sandwich? (*He takes another sandwich, sits down, all at once spills some wine, and commences violently wiping his trousers with his handkerchief*) I say, *must* we have our meal off a chest?
Brandon Here you are.

Brandon comes forward, gets Rupert another glass of wine and generally puts him right

Rupert Thank you.

Brandon goes over and fills Sir Johnstone's glass with wine

Brandon Is Lady Kentley any better, sir?
Sir Johnstone No. I'm afraid not. I'm afraid she's still in bed.
Brandon Oh. I'm sorry. And how's Ronald getting on?
Sir Johnstone Oh, Ronald? He's getting on all right. He's merely idling, of course, now, like you two.
Granillo Does he like it, or does he want to get back?
Sir Johnstone Oh, no. He doesn't want to get back. He has a great time.
Leila Who's Ronald?
Sir Johnstone Ronald? He's my son and heir. Twenty years of age.
Rupert Oh, I know Ronald. He was in the papers the other day for winning the high jump at the Varsity sports.
Sir Johnstone That's right.
Rupert Yes. I remember it well. There was a picture of me next door to it.
Sir Johnstone Oh — was there?
Rupert Yes. Not — though — for winning the high jump. Oh yes, quite an old friend.
Brandon Yes, he's a sprightly lad, is Ronald.

There is a slight pause

Raglan Brandon says he's like me. Is that true, sir?

Sir Johnstone Why, yes, he is rather like you, when you come to think of it. Quite like, really.

Raglan (*to Leila*) I've a double, apparently.

Leila My dear! How *excruciating*!

Raglan (*to Sir Johnstone*) In what way is he like me, sir?

Sir Johnstone Oh, I don't know. Just in general youthfulness — —

Brandon — and innocence, and freshness, and — —

Raglan Oh, shut up, Brandon.

Brandon He's so afraid they won't think him a man, isn't he?

Sir Johnstone That's like Ronald, too. I'm afraid they won't feel like that for long, though.

Brandon No. They won't, poor dears.

Sir Johnstone Of course, my boy is the most infantile thing in the world. I honestly believe his only passion in holiday time is the movies. When I saw him at lunch he was just *rushing* off to the Coliseum.

Granillo, at the mantelpiece, makes a movement

Brandon But that's not the movies, is it? I thought it was a music hall. Not that I know. I've never been there in my life.

Leila Never been to the Coliseum?

Rupert Why — *should* he have been to the Coliseum?

Leila Oh — I thought everybody had been.

Brandon Well — I haven't.

Granillo Neither have I. Is that the place in the Haymarket?

Leila My dear! You're mixing it up with the Capitol! What abysmal ignorance!

Granillo stands with his back to the mantelpiece, his coat open and the blue ticket protuberant in his pocket

Sir Johnstone You'd have been a sad dog as an ancient Roman, Granillo.

Rupert Yes. He would. Indeed in the days of the Caesars, the results of confusing the Coliseum with the Capitol would have been, I should imagine, almost fatal. Certainly you'd have been taken up.

Leila What *was* the Capitol, then? Wasn't it where they all got up and held forth?

Rupert The Capitol, I am told, was the Roman temple to Jupiter on the Tarpeian hill.

Leila Oh, my dear! Weren't they *sweet*!

Rupert Wherein — exactly — were the Ancient Romans "sweet"?

Leila My dear — such awful *fools*! Going in for Jupiter, and temples, and all that. Such a terrible lot of bother about *nothing*!

Sir Johnstone Well, that's one way of looking at it.

Leila Well, anyway, you must — —

Rupert But to return to the twentieth century for just one moment ... Do you mean to tell me, Granillo, that you have never been to the Coliseum?

Granillo No. Of course I haven't. Never. Why?

Rupert (*looking at Granillo*) Is that so? Dear, dear ...

Granillo Yes. Why?

Everybody is quite still

Rupert (*slowly*) You mean to say you can stand there — and puff out your chest — and tell me you have never been to the Coliseum?

Granillo Yes. Why? Why should you think that I had?

Rupert Merely the hawk-like sharpness of my vision.

Sir Johnstone Why? Is it a crime never to have been to the Coliseum?

Rupert No, sir, I don't expect it's a crime.

Sir Johnstone For in that case I am afraid I myself am guilty.

Rupert Oh, no, sir. I merely thought that Granillo — by the mere look of him, standing there in his beautiful dark blue suit — was not the sort of person who had never been to the Coliseum.

Granillo Well — I haven't.

Brandon (*moving* DS *from the sideboard*) But young Ronald has been to the Coliseum, anyway, sir?

Sir Johnstone That's right.

There is a slight pause. Leila gets up for another sandwich, and Raglan comes forward to help her

Rupert (*also moving to the chest and getting in further muddles with plates, et cetera*) You know, I'm coming to the conclusion that there's some ulterior motive about this chest picnic.

Granillo (*again a trifle too heavily*) What do you mean? Ulterior motive?

Rupert looks at Granillo without replying. He is obviously a little surprised at the other's tone

Brandon You mean it's done purely to make poor Rupert spill things over his trousers?

Rupert I think it's more than likely.

Leila Oh, I suspect much worse than that. *I* think they've committed murder, and it's simply chock-full of rotting bones. It's just the sort of thing for rotting bones, isn't it?

Raglan Yes — it is, isn't it?

Leila Yes, it is.

Brandon My dear — you're right. I wouldn't let you see the inside of that chest for worlds.
Leila I'm sure you wouldn't.

Granillo, again noticeably, walks back to his seat R

And it's all very well to try and bluff me out and pretend you're willing to let me see — —
Brandon But, my dear — that's just what I said I *wouldn't* do.
Leila I have my suspicions.
Sir Johnstone But surely your murderer, having chopped up and concealed his victim in a chest — wouldn't ask all his friends round to come and eat off it.
Rupert (*slowly*) Not unless he was a very stupid, and very conceited murderer.
Sir Johnstone Very stupid, and very conceited.
Rupert Which, of course, he might be.
Leila In fact, it's exactly what all criminals are!
Brandon Oh no, I don't think so ...

There is another pause

Leila Talking of murderers — have you seen that new thing at the New Gallery?
Raglan Yes, I saw that. Isn't it good?
Leila Yes. *Isn't* it good? I didn't like *her*, though, much — that new woman — I didn't think she was much good.
Raglan No, *she* wasn't much good. That other film was good, though, wasn't it?
Leila Yes. *Wasn't* it good?
Raglan Yes, it was good, wasn't it?
Rupert The Lord look down upon us. We have fallen amongst fans.
Leila Of course, the man I've got a passion for is William Powell.
Rupert Is *he* good? (*He looks sardonically at Leila and Raglan in turn during the following*)
Leila My dear, *absolutely marvellous*! You know, my dear — *strong, silent*. In fact, I think I like him better than John Gilbert now.
Raglan Oh, do you like John Gilbert?
Leila Oh — rather. I think he's terribly good.
Raglan Yes — he is good. Not as good as Ronald Colman, though.
Leila Oh — don't you think so? Did you see him in the old version of *The Merry Widow*?
Raglan Yes, he was good in that. Of course, he had a moustache in that, didn't he?

Rupert I expect *that* improved him, didn't it?

Leila But then John Gilbert *always* had a moustache, didn't he?

Raglan Oh no. Rather not. I've seen him in thousands of ones without. All the early ones.

Rupert (*despairingly*) The early ones!

Leila By the way, did you see Robert Montgomery in that thing with Joan Crawford? I've forgotten what it was called … "The Wonderful Something" — or something — you know — it was all sort of — *you* know …

Rupert I, for one, at the moment of speaking, do not.

Raglan Yes, I know what you mean. "The Wonderful" — I've forgotten what … It was jolly good, wasn't it? What do you think of her — Joan Crawford?

Leila (*disparagingly*) Oh — I don't know … Like all *these*, you know.

Raglan Oh — I think she's rather good.

Rupert I once went to the pictures and saw Mary Pickford.

Raglan Oh, how did you like her?

Rupert Oh, I don't know. Like all *these*, you know …

Leila What was she in, anyway?

Rupert I can't quite recall. "The Something Something", I think. Or something like that. (*Pause*) Something very like it, anyway.

Leila I don't believe you ever went.

Brandon I never knew you were a fan like this, Leila. I simply abhor the things myself.

Leila What — on moral grounds?

Brandon Oh, no. They simply make me go to sleep. And all those places are so infernally stuffy. Tell me, what do *you* think about films, Mrs Debenham?

Pause

Mrs Debenham (*snapping to attention and smirking*) No — I don't …

Silence. Everybody looks at each other, inclined to giggle

Leila Well, if you'd seen — —

Rupert (*cutting in*) Pardon me. I cannot quite ascertain Mrs Debenham's opinion. She says she doesn't. Does she mean that she does not think about films, or merely that she does not think at all?

Pause

Mrs Debenham Oh, yes. Decidedly.

Rupert Ah. I see.

Brandon (*rising and placing his plate upon the chest with an air of finality*) Well, anyway, who says books?

Sir Johnstone (*rising*) Ay.

Leila Yes, that's a very good idea.

Brandon (*looking at Leila*) I have a gramophone for the very young, if they care to make use of it.

Leila But I thought you said the room was covered with books.

Brandon Oh, no — there's room to dance.

Raglan (*looking at the wireless cabinet*) Hallo, you've got a wireless, I see.

Brandon Yes. So we have. (*He goes over to the wireless*) Let's see what they're doing. They won't be dancing yet. (*He switches on the apparatus*)

Leila Oh, no. Not till eleven.

Pause

Brandon Hallo — it's not doing anything.

Rupert Then take it off. (*He rises, moves to the fire, takes a cigarette and lights it. He leans on the mantelpiece*)

Brandon switches off the radio, takes Sir Johnstone by the arm and leads him towards the door

Brandon This way, Sir Johnstone. (*He frees his arm at the doorway, and turns to Mrs Debenham*) Will you come along, too, Mrs Debenham? *You* dance, don't you?

Mrs Debenham Oh, I really couldn't say!

Rupert We never know until we try, do we?

Mrs Debenham I beg your pardon.

Rupert Granted — utterly.

Brandon Well, come along, the rest of you — if you want to, that is. I've dozens of records in here.

Brandon, Sir Johnstone and Mrs Debenham exit

Raglan and Leila stand. Raglan rather ostentatiously holds back the door for Leila

Leila (*smiling up at Raglan*) Thank you.

Raglan and Leila exit

Granillo and Rupert are left alone. Granillo moves over to Rupert at the mantelpiece and takes another cigarette. He stands us *of Rupert*

Granillo (*slapping Rupert affectionately upon the shoulder*) Well, Rupert?
Rupert Well? *You* look rather fagged out.
Granillo Do I? I don't feel it.
Rupert What have you been doing with yourself?
Granillo (*yet again too heavily*) Doing with myself? Nothing. Why do you ask?
Rupert For no reason whatever, my dear Granno. You seem rather touchy.
Granillo Yes. I'm a bit liverish. I've been sleeping most of the afternoon, and that always puts me out for the rest of the day.
Rupert Ah, that's what *I* do …

In the room across the passage the gramophone begins

Granillo Writing anything lately?
Rupert (*reflectively*) Yes … A little thing about doves — and a little thing about rain — both good. Very good, in fact … And then, of course, I'm getting ahead with the big work …
Granillo That going well?
Rupert Yes. Very. Indeed, it promises to be not only the best thing I have ever written, but the best thing I have ever read. (*He nods his head to the gramophone*) This is rather nice, isn't it?

Granillo suddenly yawns, sticking out his chest and lifting his hands. The blue Coliseum slip is prominent in his waistcoat. He resumes a normal position, leaning against the mantelpiece. Rupert leans against the mantelpiece, close to Granillo and looking at him

Rupert So you and Brandon leave tonight for Oxford?
Granillo (*looking into the fire*) That's right.
Rupert What time are you going?
Granillo We're aiming to start about ten-thirty.
Rupert Arriving there about when?
Granillo Oh. About three. Why?
Rupert Peculiar form of enjoyment, Granno. But, then, that's like you.
Granillo Why? Lovely moonlight night.
Rupert It's not. It's raining already.
Granillo It's not.
Rupert Yes, it is. (*He raises his hand*) Listen.

The rain can be heard pouring gently down. The gramophone stops in the next room, and there is a sudden great quiet over everything. Granillo listens, first by putting his head slightly sideways, and then by suddenly turning his head to look at the window. In this instant, Rupert makes a deft snatch at the little ticket in Granillo's waistcoat pocket, then holds his hand behind his back rather awkwardly. Granillo turns his head back and sees Rupert with his hand behind his back but Rupert puts his hand in his pocket in quite an easy fashion, and Granillo passes it over. But there has been a queer little pause

Granillo (*looking into the fireplace again*) Yes, it *is* coming down, isn't it?
Rupert (*spotting a book on the mantelpiece and reaching for it*) What have we here? ... Ah-ha! ... Conrad. Dear me ... Dear me ... (*He turns the pages interestedly*)

The gramophone starts up again. Suddenly the door across the passage opens and the sound of the gramophone comes loudly through, also laughter and voices

Brandon (*off*) Granno!
Granillo Hallo?
Brandon (*off*) *Granno*! You're *wanted*!
Granillo Coming! (*To Rupert*) Coming along?
Rupert No, I'm all right.

Granillo exits

Rupert, left alone, goes on reading the book for a little. Then, still standing and holding the book, he fishes in his left-hand pocket for his spectacle case, taking the spectacles out and looking at the book at the same time. Then he strolls towards the armchair. He sits down and adjusts the spectacles on his face, still reading. He puts the spectacle case absently on the table, and fishes in another pocket for the blue ticket. He holds the ticket out, straightening it on his knee as he goes on reading. Then he closes the book with one hand and places it on the table, leans back and gives his whole attention to the ticket. He turns it over, looking at each side, then screws it up in his hand. He drops his hand over the side of the armchair, and looks thoughtfully − not suspiciously − ahead of him. Rupert stays like this for nearly half a minute. Then he takes up book again and makes to start reading

Sabot enters

Rupert (*looking up*) Ah − good-evening, Sabot.
Sabot Good-evening, sair. (*He clears the meal away on to the tray during the following*)
Rupert (*reading*) How are you getting on?
Sabot Very well, thank you, sair.

There is a pause. The sound of the rain becomes louder

Rupert (*after a pause; quietly*) It's going to be a dirty night.
Sabot Yes, sair. It's set in now, sair.
Rupert I suppose Mr Brandon'll still be going, though.
Sabot Pardon, sair?
Rupert I suppose Mr Brandon'll still be going, though — to Oxford?
Sabot Oh — yes, sair. I suppose so, sair.

Sabot busies himself with clearing. He picks up a large pile of plates. Rupert all at once puts the book down and looks at the little ticket again

Rupert Have you any idea of the date, Sabot?
Sabot Ze date, sair? Yes, sair. It ees zee — er — (*screwing up his eyes*) er — sixteenth, sair.
Rupert The — ? (*He is about to repeat "the sixteenth" in surprise*)
Sabot (*quickly*) No, sair! No, sair! It ees not, sair! It ees the *seventeenth*, sair!
Rupert (*looking quite openly at the ticket*) Yes. I thought so. The seventeenth.

Pause

Rupert Have you been getting into trouble lately, Sabot?
Sabot Trouble, sair?
Rupert Yes. Trouble.
Sabot Er … *Trouble*, sair?
Rupert Uncanny as it may seem, the word I employed, Sabot, was trouble.
Sabot Er … What kind of trouble, sair?
Rupert Why — have you a selection?
Sabot Ah, sair. Life. She is full of trouble.
Rupert She certainly is. Indeed she is almost unintermittently troublesome. I was wondering, though, whether you had been getting into any trouble with your employers.
Sabot Me, sair? No, sair. What should make you think so, sair?
Rupert Well, I telephoned this house at a quarter to eight and heard the most hysterical noises.
Sabot Hysterical noises, sair?
Rupert Hysterical — Sabot — noises. Somebody had evidently lost their nerve. I was wondering whether you were the cause of it.
Sabot Me, sair? No, sair. Not me, sair. I was not here till five to nine.

There is a long pause. Sabot continues clearing the meal away

Rupert Then are *you* the one that frequents the Coliseum, Sabot?

Sabot (*not having heard, or understood, and merely being polite*) Yes, sair.
Rupert (*seeing that this is the wrong reply, and looking up*) I said, are *you* the one that frequents the Coliseum?
Sabot (*pulling himself together*) Oh, sair! I did not hear, sair! Pardon, sair. The Coliseum, sair? No, sair.
Rupert You don't?
Sabot Zee — er — zee music-hall, sair?
Rupert Yes.
Sabot (*in a puzzled fashion, as though accused, and quite innocently*) No, sair … No, sair. I have been there once, sair … Many years ago, sair.
Rupert But not lately?
Sabot No, sair.

There is another pause. Sabot goes on clearing

Rupert Then is it Mr Granillo who frequents the Coliseum?
Sabot Mr Granillo, sair?
Rupert Or is it Mr Brandon who frequents the place?
Sabot Mr Brandon, sair?

Brandon enters. He is quite bright and cheerful, and moves straight over to the sideboard, plainly to fetch drinks

Brandon (*as he moves; rallyingly*) Hallo! Hallo! "Mr Brandon"? What's all this about, Mr Brandon?
Rupert (*quickly*) I was asking the good Sabot, Brandon, whether Mr Brandon would still travel to Oxford in all this rain. Wasn't I, Sabot?
Sabot (*looking up quickly from Brandon to Rupert, in a puzzled way*) Er … Yes, sair. Yes, sair.
Brandon (*bending down to fish in the cupboard in the sideboard for bottles*) Well — I hope he told you that we are. What's a little rain, anyway? (*He produces a bottle of whisky and looks at it, walking to the door*) Besides, we've got nobody to look after us here. One moment, I'll be back in a minute. (*He suddenly turns DS to look over Rupert's shoulder to see what he is reading*) What's he reading? *The Rover.* I'll be back in a minute. Why don't you come in? (*He turns to Sabot*) That's all right, Sabot. You can go straight away now — now that's cleared.
Sabot Thank you, sair.
Brandon (*to Rupert*) Back in a minute.

Brandon exits

There is another pause as Sabot puts the final touch to his clearing

Rupert That, Sabot, was what we call a White One.
Sabot (*again uncomprehending*) A White One, sair? (*Understanding*) Oh, sair! Yes, sair … A white one, sair. (*He draws air in through his teeth rather nervously*)

Rupert goes on reading

Sabot moves to the door and opens it, then comes back and fetches the tray containing everything cleared, and exits with it into the passage, leaving the door open. He can be heard putting the tray outside. He comes back to close the door, but pauses in the doorway and bows

Bonsoir, monsieur.
Rupert (*looking up from the book*) Good-night, Sabot.

Sabot exits

There is a pause. The rain comes down

Rupert abruptly closes the book, gets up and moves towards the window. He pauses at the chest and gives it a kick — not very suspiciously, but curiously, in passing — goes on to the window and looks out. Rain. He moves DS and helps himself to a drink, then goes back to the same chair and resumes his book. He suddenly closes it and looks in front of him for about ten seconds. He makes to resume the book

A chorus of voices is heard from the next room

Brandon enters

Brandon (*looking at the chest and at Rupert*) Hallo, Sabot gone?
Rupert Yes, Sabot gone. (*He puts the book on the table*) Brandon.

Brandon closes the door and moves to the mantelpiece for a cigarette. He lights one

Pause. Rupert settles himself in the armchair

Brandon Um? (*He pokes the fire during the following*)
Rupert I have just thought of something rather queer.
Brandon Something queer. What's that?
Rupert All this talk about rotting bones in chests … (*He gazes lethargically into the distance*)

Brandon stands up, poker in hand, and looks at Rupert

The gramophone is suddenly heard again, together with a great guffaw of general laughter

CURTAIN

ACT II

The scene is the same as before, and no time has elapsed. The offstage gramophone takes up where it left off

Brandon (*in the same attitude*) Talk about rotting bones in chests, Rupert?

Rupert Yes.

Brandon What about them? (*He turns round and pokes the fire again during Rupert's line*)

Rupert Do you remember when you were an infant, Brandon?

Brandon M'm ... (*He finishes poking the fire, puts the poker back and wipes his hands on his handkerchief during the following*)

Rupert And how you used to tell me stories round the fire?

Brandon Yes. Rather. I remember.

Rupert Do you remember your chest complex, Brandon?

Brandon My chest complex?

Rupert Yes. Whatever the story was — piratical, detective, murder, adventure or ghost — it always contained a marvellous denouement with a bloody chest containing corpses. You had a perfect mania for it, don't you remember?

Brandon (*suddenly a trifle serious, forgetting himself*) Yes, I'd forgotten that.

Rupert looks at Brandon. There is a pause

Rupert Why *should* you have remembered it?

Brandon (*putting his handkerchief away and walking over to the sideboard for whisky*) Yes, it's quite true. I remember now. What about it, though?

Rupert (*lightly*) Oh, nothing. Just queer, that's all. You were a morbid child.

Brandon (*pouring out whisky; quietly*) How queer — exactly?

Rupert Oh, just queer. Us all talking tonight about rotting bones in chests. It just came back to me, that's all.

Brandon (*intent upon pouring, and as though suddenly seeing the light*) Oh! I see what you mean! Yes! Are you going to have some of this, Rupert?

Rupert What's that? Whisky? Yes. Thank you. (*He makes to stand*)

Brandon All right! Don't get up. I'll bring it over ... (*He pours whisky into a second glass*) Say when ...

Rupert gives instructions as Brandon pours

Rupert When. No. A little more. When. When!

Brandon brings Rupert's drink over to him

   Thank you.
Brandon (*holding up his glass*) Happy days.
Rupert How's the old man getting on with his books?
Brandon Going to take the entire library away with him, as far as I can see.
   I'm simply saying goodbye to it.
Rupert I didn't know you were a book collector.
Brandon I've only been one for about a year.
Rupert What exactly is your line?
Brandon Well — I've theories about some of the Victorians. Everything
   comes round, you know, in time.
Rupert For example … ?
Brandon For example? Well — Matthew Arnold, Carlyle, and people of
   that sort.
Rupert Matthew Arnold, perhaps.
Brandon What's wrong with Carlyle, anyway?
Rupert My dear Brandon. An unspeakable person. Pull yourself together.
Brandon Oh, I don't agree with you. He's got guts, anyway.
Rupert (*screwing up his face*) Guts!
Brandon And a kind of angry righteousness, which you don't get nowadays.
Rupert Thank God!
Brandon (*swilling down the remains of his whisky*) Well. I must go in and
   function. Aren't you coming?
Rupert (*getting up*) Yes.

The gramophone is heard again

   Ah — I like that one. (*Beating time*) Dee-de-dee-de-dee-dedeedee. (*He
   moves to the door*) I say. What's the time? (*He compares his watch with
   the grandfather clock*) I want to be home fairly early tonight.
Brandon Plenty of time. Come along.(*He switches off the lamp and the
   overhead lights*)

   Brandon and Rupert exit together

*The room is in darkness except for a gleam of light round the door from the
passage*

Brandon (*off*) Now I've left the cigarettes. Go along in, Rupert. I'll be in in
   a moment.

Brandon enters, his figure being silhouetted against the doorway as he comes in

There are voices from the next room as Rupert enters it

Brandon moves down to the mantelpiece for cigarettes. There is a pause. He suddenly moves over to the window and draws the curtains back. He is silhouetted against the window's light

The rain is heard, and seen, beating against the windows

Brandon moves down to the chest and stands by it. He sits on it, and bends down to the lock

The gramophone in the next room ceases. There is a pause. Suddenly the light in the passage goes off, and then on again

The figure on the chest becomes upright and tense. Pause

All at once Granillo's figure is seen against the light of the doorway. He closes the door. He is inside the darkened room

The figure on the chest remains motionless. Granillo moves towards the chest. Pause. Granillo touches Brandon and lets out a horrible, shuddering, muffled scream

Brandon (*crying out*) Damnation!

Granillo's scream dies down into a sobbing noise

Brandon, cursing furiously, gets down from the chest with a heavy thud and rushes over to the little lamp on the table and switches it on

(*Blazing*) What in God's name do you mean?

Granillo sinks down by the chest with his arms on it

Granillo Oh — oh! Oh, God!
Brandon (*fiercely*) What's the matter, man? Tell me what's the matter!
Granillo (*his voice coming from within his folded arms*) I thought it was him. I thought it was him! I thought it was Ronald!

Brandon switches the main light on and the lamp off, then goes over to the sideboard and pours out a large whisky and soda, spilling some of it over. He brings the whisky over to Granillo

Brandon For God's sake, drink that.

Granillo takes the whisky and sips it feebly

Be quick — be quick, man!

Granillo Why were you sitting there? Why were you trying to frighten me?

Brandon I wasn't trying to frighten you. I was wondering what you were up to. I wasn't even sure it was you. Why did you want to sneak in like that? You got what you deserved. Hang you — you've upset me.

Granillo I wanted to see that everything was all right. I'm sorry. My nerve's going. I'm all right. I'll be all right. (*He finishes the rest of the whisky with a gulp, and makes a wry face as it goes down*) I'll be all right. Give me some more of that.

Brandon (*taking Granillo's glass*) Get up, get up! (*He pours Granillo some more whisky*)

Granillo gets up and sits on the chest. Brandon gives him another glass full of whisky and soda

I'm going into the other room. Come in when you can. (*He moves to the door and pauses there*) Don't get drunk on that.

Granillo No.

Brandon exits with the cigarettes, closing the door. Pause

Granillo looks in front of him. He swills off the remainder of his whisky at one gulp again. There is a pause; he looks in front of him. He goes to the sideboard and helps himself to another large glass of whisky and soda. He takes a sip and moves slowly down to the fireplace, giving a little stagger of drunkenness just before reaching it. He leans against the mantelpiece, looking into the fire. He slowly turns round and looks at the chest. He quickly takes another long gulp at his whisky, pulls a long face and coughs. The cough continues horribly; he cannot leave off. He stops to gasp, and then starts again

Brandon enters hurriedly

Brandon (*looking at Granillo*) What's the matter, man?

Granillo (*straining*) Cough. (*He coughs again, continuing through the following*)

Brandon Pull yourself together. Come on. Come on. You can stop if you want to. (*He thuds Granillo on the back*) Come on.

Granillo's coughing slowly dies out

Granillo All right. It went down the wrong way. (*He now seems quite calm again in every way*) What are you back here for? (*He sits down*)
Brandon They want those Beethoven records. You know. those old ones. I couldn't find them in there. You had them last, didn't you? Are they in here, or upstairs?
Granillo Oh, yes. They're upstairs in my room.
Brandon I'll go and get them. Where are they?
Granillo They'll be a hell of a nuisance to get at. They're at the bottom of my trunk.
Brandon What? The green one?
Granillo Yes. But they're right at the bottom, and it's locked. Must they have their Beethoven records?
Brandon All right, then. You come and tell them. (*He moves down to the fire, puts coal on it and pokes it*) You're all right, aren't you?
Granillo (*rising and going to the door*) Yes. Quite. (*He opens the door and makes to leave*)
Brandon (*still poking the fire*) One moment, Granno.

Granillo stops

Granillo Yes.
Brandon Shut the door.
Granillo (*shutting it*) Yes.
Brandon You've got that little ticket, haven't you? You'd better give it to me and we'll destroy it right away now.
Granillo What ticket?
Brandon Ronald's ticket.
Granillo (*vaguely, only half-realizing the significance of what he has been asked*) What Ronald's ticket?
Brandon (*tersely, yet still quite coolly*) Oh, don't dither, Granno. Ronald's ticket, Ronald's Coliseum ticket.
Granillo Ronald's Coliseum ticket?
Brandon Sh! Not so loud, you fool. Yes.
Granillo I haven't got the Coliseum ticket.
Brandon Don't be a fool, Granno. I gave it to you.
Granillo You didn't give it to me.
Brandon (*clenching his hands and looking at Granillo*) Granno!
Granillo (*almost simultaneously*) Wait!

Granillo plunges his thumb into the waistcoat pocket where the ticket was. Pause. He does the same with the other thumb in the opposite pocket. Pause. He checks the right waistcoat pocket beneath then, quickly, the left. He looks at Brandon

Brandon Granno!

Granillo goes through all four waistcoat pockets again rapidly and in a panic. He looks at Brandon. He goes through his two coat pockets, then his inside pockets and trousers pockets. He turns his trousers pockets out, then checks his coat pockets again. He comes back to his waistcoat pockets

Granillo You didn't — —
Brandon Hip! Hip! ... Hip pocket!

Granillo feels in his hip pocket, with the same result

Granillo You didn't — —
Brandon Look again! Look again!

Granillo repeats the entire performance, which lasts nearly a minute. This time, also, he brings out his wallet and looks in that

Granillo (*hoarsely*) You didn't give it to me. I never had it.
Brandon (*looking at Granillo with a kind of calm rage*) I gave it into your hand.
Granillo You didn't. I never had it.
Brandon I gave it into your hand!
Granillo See if you've got it.
Brandon I haven't got it, I tell you. Where is it?

Brandon moves towards the sideboard and rapidly and desperately searches himself with his back to the audience. He bangs on the chest with sudden terrible rage

Where is it? Where is it? Where is it? (*He stands still, both hands still on the chest*)
Granillo Shshshsh! I put it in my waistcoat pocket.

Rupert enters during the next line and stands in the doorway

Brandon (*shouting*) You put it in your waistcoat pocket! You put it in your waistcoat pocket! Where is it *now*? Where is it *now*?
Rupert My dear Brandon. What *have* you lost?

There is a long pause. Brandon and Granillo glare into Rupert's eyes, and he looks coolly at them

Brandon (*his hands still on the chest*) My temper, Rupert. Sorry, Granno.

Granillo (*moving over to pour himself another drink; very nervously*) That's all right.

Rupert Oh — (*hobbling* DC) I hope I'm not interfering.

Brandon (*moving to the fireplace and lighting a cigarette*) No. It's my fault. You didn't know that Granno and I behaved like that, did you, Rupert? But we often have outbursts, like this — and always about trifles, eh, Granno?

Granillo Yes. (*He drinks*)

Brandon On this occasion it was a question of a case of Beethoven gramophone records, which poor old Granno couldn't produce. I was chiding him for his remissness. The party'll have to do without its Beethoven tonight.

Rupert Well, it's an ill wind that blows nobody any good. What a queer thing to quarrel about.

Brandon Yes. But we do quarrel about queer things nowadays, don't we, Granno?

Granillo We do.

Rupert (*sitting down*) Can I have another drink, please?

Granillo, preoccupied, does not respond

Brandon Granno.

Granillo Yes. Whisky?

Rupert Yes, please.

Granillo pours a whisky for Rupert and brings it over to him. His hand is trembling violently as he gives the drink to Rupert, and this does not go by unobserved

Rupert Can I have some soda?

Granillo Oh. Sorry. (*He moves back and pours soda into the glass, then returns with it to Rupert*)

Rupert Thank you. Ever so much. (*He drinks*)

Granillo returns to the sideboard during the following

(*After a pause*) Well, as a matter of fact, I'm in here on an errand.

Brandon An errand?

Rupert Yes. I want some rope.

Brandon }
Granillo } (*together*) Rope!

Rupert Yes. Why so excited? Rope. The young people in the other room, having exhausted the lyric possibilities of the gramophone, are now projecting their entire youthful *élan* and ingenuity into the composition of a parcel. And they want something to do it up with.

Brandon A parcel?
Rupert Yes. The old man's books. You'd better see what goes into it. I'm
    sure he's lifting all your best.

There is a sudden tremendous clap of thunder

    Hallo — here we are …

There is another clap, which dies down into the distance

    I thought it was coming.

*There is an enormous downpour of rain. Brandon moves to the window and
looks out*

Brandon Damnation … Yes, it's coming down all right.
Rupert Surely — —

*There is another, even more tremendous clap of thunder, which causes
Rupert to rise to his feet*

Granillo drops a full glass on the floor

Granillo Blast! (*He tries to mop the spillage up with his handkerchief but
    gets into difficulties*) Oh, where are the servants? Where are the servants?

*Rupert looks at Granillo in a surprised way then moves over to look out of
the window*

    My dear Brandon, surely you're not going in this?
Brandon (*also looking out of the window*) Oh yes, we'll go all right. It'll clear
    up soon.

There is another clap of thunder. Pause

    Besides, we've got nowhere to sleep here. The beds are all dismantled.
Rupert (*moving* DS *again*) Oh, that needn't worry you. You can come round
    and put up with me if you care. I've plenty of room.
Brandon (*moving* DS *and putting his arm round Rupert*) No — thank you,
    old boy. I think we'll try and make it.
Rupert Very well, have it your own way.

Brandon moves to the fireplace during the following

Leila and Raglan burst in. Raglan is carrying books and is behind Leila

Leila Hallo! Did you hear that?

Rupert M'm. We heard it all right. We're scared out of our wits.

Leila I *know*! (*She goes to the window*) And it's simply coming down in *sheets*! Surely you're not going to Oxford tonight?

Granillo Certainly we are.

Leila But, my dear, you *can't*! You'll be simply *swamped out*, my dear! *Flooded*, my dear!

Brandon I hear you want some string, Leila.

Leila Oh, yes — so we do! (*She turns to Raglan*) Where are the books? Oh, here we are. We're going to make a parcel, my dear. Come on. (*She takes half the books from Raglan and plonks them down on the chest*) We've got some paper. (*To Raglan again*) Have you got the paper?

Raglan Oh, no, I've forgotten the paper.

Leila Well, go and get it! Be quick!

Raglan Right you are.

Raglan exits

Brandon (*moving to the door and shouting*) And you might bring the cigarettes while you're there, Kenneth!

Raglan (*off*) Right you are!

Brandon returns to the fire. Rupert goes up to the chest and looks at the books during the following

Leila (*moving to the wireless*) Can I see what's on?

Brandon Certainly.

Leila touches the indicators. Nothing happens. There is a pause for about ten seconds

Rupert This, of course, is the time when I really enjoy the wireless.

Leila That's the storm, I expect.

Raglan enters with paper and cigarettes. He hands the cigarettes to Brandon

Raglan Here you are.

Brandon Ta.

Raglan (*giving the paper to Leila*) Here you are.

Leila Thanks. Well, now we want the string. Where's the string?

Brandon Oh — the string's in the other room. I'll get it.
Raglan (*obviously enjoying himself and frantically eager to serve*) No, no.
I'll get it. Where is it?
Brandon It's in the sort of big vase thing — *you* know.
Leila Do you know the sort of big vase thing?
Raglan Oh, yes — I know. I'll get it.

Raglan rushes out again

Rupert (*looking up from his book and straight at Leila for a moment;
mockingly*) Isn't he *sweet?*
Leila Yes, he is rather a lamb. (*She spreads the paper out on the chest during
the following*)
Rupert (*putting his book down*) Yes. (*He hobbles over to the chair* L) A
decided duck. (*He sits down*)

Raglan returns with a ball of string

Raglan Here we are.

*Raglan gives Leila the string. She arranges books on the paper and he stands
over her, helpfully*

(*Turning to Brandon*) Oh! And Sir Johnstone wants to know whether
he can browse on that sort of top shelf thing — I didn't quite follow
what he — —
Brandon Oh, yes. I know what he means.

Granillo moves to get another drink

(*Noticing Granillo's move; to Granillo*) I say, Granno, do go in and explain
to him. The poor old man's getting into hopeless muddles.

*Granillo, at the sideboard, swiftly pours and swallows a drink. then moves
towards the door. Walking unsteadily, he happens to stumble against the
chest*

Granillo exits a little insecurely

There is a slight pause and silence

Leila (*rolling her eyes*) Just a *little* … I think?
Rupert I should say completely.

Brandon What? Granno blotto? Yes. He is a bit. It's this whisky.

There is another growl of thunder

Raglan Hallo, listen. Here we are again.
Leila (*looking behind her*) Oh, my hat!
Brandon I believe you're afraid of storms, Leila.
Leila My dear! I am. I simply rush round in circles. It's hereditary, you know. You should see my mother.
Rupert What does she rush around in?
Leila My dear! She doesn't! She simply hides herself in cupboards.
Brandon Really?
Leila (*taking the string from Raglan*) All entangled in the linen, my dear! If it comes on again, you'll probably all see me suddenly take a *violent plunge* into this chest. (*She busies herself with the string during the following*)
Raglan I should love to see that.
Leila Head-foremost, my dear! By the way, can you get into this chest, or is it locked?

The remark goes unanswered. Brandon lights a cigarette and pretends not to hear. There is a pause

Rupert (*repeating Leila's words carefully, looking at Brandon*) Can you get into this chest, Brandon, or is it locked?
Brandon (*pretending that he has not heard*) What? Oh! Yes, you can get into it if you want to.
Leila Oh, well, then *I'm* safe.
Rupert (*looking at the chest from his chair*) Isn't there a lock on that, though?

Pause

Brandon Yes. There is.
Leila (*suddenly and brightly*) Oh, my dear! You've forgotten! (*She hands the ball of string back to Raglan*) He's got his murdered man in here!
Raglan Oh, so he has! We'd forgotten that, hadn't we?
Leila Well, *you* may have. *I* hadn't. I say, can I have another spot?
Brandon I'm sorry, Leila. (*He moves over to the sideboard*) And you too, Kenneth?
Raglan Well — I think I would — really …
Leila (*tugging at the string*) Yes, that's what he's been committing (*tug*) — murder (*tug*) … (*To Raglan*) Finger, please.

Raglan puts his finger on the string

No — here. That's right. And we've caught him (*tug*) — red (*tug*) — handed.

Brandon (*jokingly and easily*) Ah, Leila. You don't know how near the mark you are.

Leila Oh — don't I? I know exactly what's inside this chest.

Brandon What?

Leila There's an old, old man. You picked him up selling papers in the street, and you did him to death for the gold fillings in his teeth. You've a lust for gold, my dear.

Brandon Oh — I see you've been following me.

Leila (*looking at the lock and fumbling with it*) No. It *is* locked, *isn't* it? And why a padlock? What *have* you got in it?

Brandon But you know, Leila. You have already explained to us what is in it.

Leila No. (*Working on the parcel again*) I honestly think you ought to let us have a look. Have you got the key?

Brandon Yes. I've got the key. It's in my waistcoat pocket.

Leila Well — hand it over and let's have a look inside.

Brandon I'm hanged if I do.

Leila But why *not*, my dear? If you're (*tug*) — really (*tug*) — innocent — you can prove it, dear.

Brandon But how often have I to tell you, Leila, that I am *not* innocent? My hands are red with a crime committed less than three hours ago.

Leila Oh, well — if you won't (*she tugs the string and hurts her finger*) — damn — you *won't*. All the same, if I had strong men about me, they'd force it from you.

Raglan I'll be your strong man.

Leila Will you? All right. Go and be strong.

Raglan How do I do that?

Leila Oh — that's up to you.

Raglan (*moving* DS) All right, then. (*He strikes an attitude*) Now then, Mr Brandon, hand it over, or it will be the worse for you.

Leila Said he, eyeing the other fearlessly.

Brandon Come and get it, Kenneth.

Raglan (*a little nervously, and rather wishing he hadn't begun it*) Which pocket is it in?

Brandon Top. Right.

Raglan Mine or yours?

Brandon Mine.

Leila Go on. Seize it.

Raglan I'll give him ten seconds, shall I?

Leila That's right.

Brandon Right you are. Ten seconds.

Leila One — two — three …
Raglan (*creeping a little nearer*) Won't you surrender?
Brandon No.
Leila Four — five — —

Raglan creeps nearer still

— six — seven …

Raglan suddenly makes a spring at Brandon, who is not ready for him

Hooray!

Raglan and Brandon begin to wrestle, both with a smile on their faces, but looking a little breathless and anxious

Rupert watches carefully

The struggle becomes a little too protracted

My dears! What *will* men not do for me!

The struggle becomes a little more breathless, and even unfriendly. Raglan looks for a moment as though he is going to get the best of it

Slaughtering each other, of course!

They continue. All at once, Brandon seizes Raglan's wrist and has him at his mercy. Brandon gives the wrist a violent twist, looking, suddenly, entirely malicious

Raglan (*unexpectedly, actually shouting*) Ow!

Brandon still grips Raglan's wrist

Rupert (*now startled by the sheer noise*) Mr Raglan, we cannot on every occasion be Strong, but it is always possible to be Silent. What *is* he doing to you?
Raglan (*released by Brandon*) I thought he'd bust my arm. I say, Brandon, you don't know your own strength, you know. (*Rubbing his arm*) You gave me an awful foul tug.
Brandon Kenneth. I'm profoundly sorry. Really.
Raglan No. That's all right. (*Moving to Leila again*) That's what you used to do to me at school … (*To Leila*) So I'm not your Strong Man after all.

Leila Never mind. You come back to the Mother Heart. I think he's a beast.

Brandon No, Leila. Only a desperate criminal, that's all. You must forgive me.

Leila All right. I'll forgive you. There was room in her heart even for the lowest of God's creatures — a criminal and an outcast ...

Rupert How fearfully interested in crime we all seem tonight. Why poor Brandon can't be allowed to commit his own murders in quiet I don't know.

Leila Ah, but I'm a sleuth. I'm professionally interested, you see.

Raglan Pearl White?

Leila Yes. That's right. Pearl White. Besides, it's a simple question of bringing assassins to justice.

Rupert Oh — how would you do that?

Leila Why — by having them arrested, of course.

Rupert Oh — would that do it? I have heard of assassins being brought to the Old Bailey, but I have seldom heard of them being brought to justice. I hope you're not confusing the two.

Leila Well, what's wrong with the Old Bailey, anyway?

Rupert My dear Leila, its blemish is single but ineradicable. It is human. Justice is not.

Brandon Hear, hear!

Raglan Oh, I say — are you one of these people who don't approve of capital punishment?

Rupert I think, possibly, I approve of murder too much to approve of capital punishment.

Leila
Raglan } (*together*) Approve of murder!

Brandon looks at Rupert sharply

Rupert My dear Leila, there are *so* many people that I would *so* willingly murder — *particularly* the members of my own family — and *including* the aunt so felicitously described by Mr Raglan as living in Bayswater — that it would be positively disingenuous to say that I don't approve of murder. Furthermore, I have already committed murder myself.

Brandon How do you get that?

Rupert It is all simply a question of scale. You, my friends, have, paradoxically, a horror of murder on a small scale, a veneration for it on a large scale. That is the difference between what we call murder and war. One gentleman murders another in a back alleyway in London for, let us say, since you have suggested it, the gold fillings in his teeth, and all society shrieks out for revenge upon the miscreant. They call that murder. But when the entire youth and manhood of a whole nation rises up to slaughter the entire youth and manhood of another, not even for the gold fillings in each other's teeth, then society condones and applauds the outrage, and calls it war. How, then, can I say that I disapprove of murder, seeing that I have, in the last Great War, acted on these assumptions myself? A lamentable thing, certainly, and responsible for the fact that tonight, instead of being able to fool around the gramophone with you two — a thing I should very much like to have done — I have to hobble about like an old man, on one leg. But the point is that I have proved that I don't disapprove of murder. Haven't I?

Leila No. You've done nothing of the sort. You'd be the first to be horrified by murder if it happened under your own nose.

Rupert I wonder. (*Pause*)

Leila Besides, you must have *some* moral standards.

Rupert Must I? I don't recall any.

Leila Don't be absurd. You wouldn't hurt a fly.

Rupert Wouldn't I? I've hurt thousands in my time.

There is a pause. Rupert and Leila begin talking at the same time

Leila } (*together*) { Well, I call — —
Rupert }   { Anyway, perhaps — —

Leila No, do go on.

Rupert No, do go on, please.

Leila No, do go on.

Rupert } (*together*) { All I was going to say — —
Leila }   { I was merely about to — —

Rupert I'm very sorry.

Leila No, do go on.

Rupert Shall we toss up?

Leila Well, all I was going to say — —

Rupert Yes?

Leila All I was going to say is, that I call that a jolly good parcel. (*She holds up her parcel*)

Brandon Excellent.

Leila Well, *now* what were you going to say?

Rupert I've really no idea … What are your own moral standards, then, Leila?

Leila Mine?

Brandon Oh, Leila believes in the Ten Commandments, doesn't she?

Rupert Oh, no. Surely not.

Raglan Why, what's wrong with the Ten Commandments?

Rupert Nothing whatever. Indeed, I have no doubt that they were of the profoundest significance to the nomadic needs of the tribe to whom they

were delivered. Their inadequacy and irrelevance for today, though, must
be sufficient to condemn them. I have often attempted to discover whether
it is within the range of any of us to observe each one of them. Honour my
father and mother, of course I do. How could I do otherwise? Indeed, on
the occasion of my birthday, I have never failed to send them a telegram
of congratulation. Though whether this will make my days any longer in
the land which has been given us must remain in doubt. But look at the
others. Keep holy the Sabbath day. I don't. Take not the name of the Lord
in vain. I do. Thou shalt not murder. But I have done murder, as I have
explained.

Brandon And the seventh, Rupert?

Rupert Committed. Since infancy. (*Pause*) Thou shalt not steal. But
property itself, as Proudhon has explained to us, is theft. And I am a man
of property. Moreover, these are your matches. (*He produces a box of
matches*) Indeed the only clause I am sincerely capable of adhering to is the
little stricture concerning my neighbour's ox and my neighbour's ass. Few
and far between as are my neighbours who own oxes, and fewer and farther
between as are my neighbours who own asses, I honestly think I could face
either type, in an emergency, with a pure heart. But then it might be
different if I lived in a rural district.

Leila Well, anyway, I still say that you'd never commit a murder. Your
conscience wouldn't let you.

Rupert Ah, but have I a conscience?

Brandon He's quite right. And for one who hasn't a conscience, I can
understand murder being an entirely engrossing adventure.

Rupert You mean a motiveless murder?

Brandon Yes.

Raglan Yes. That really does happen sometimes, doesn't it? You do get
people who murder purely sort of for the fun of the thing, don't you?

Leila What a peculiar idea of fun.

Raglan No, but I've heard of cases like that.

Rupert Certainly you have. And I for one can certainly enter into the
excitement of it. The only trouble about that sort of thing is that you're
bound to be found out.

Brandon (*rather too quickly*) Why should you be found out?

Pause

Rupert Because, dear Brandon, that sort of murder would not be a
motiveless murder at all. It would have a quite clear motive. Vanity. It
would be a murder of vanity. And because of that, the criminal would be
quite unable to keep from talking about it, or showing it off — in *some*
fantastic way or another. The trouble with that sort of murderer is that he

can't keep quiet about it. He won't hide it up. He wants to boast about it — and say something — do something — it may be something only just slightly *outré* — which gives him away. They have always done it and they always will.

Brandon But then suppose your murderer — your really ideal, brilliantly clever and competent murderer — a genius at it, I mean — suppose he was alive to the fact that vanity was the Achilles heel to the thing, and went specially out of his way to see that he wasn't caught like that. I'm talking of a genius at it.

Rupert (*looking at him*) Oh yes. But then he'd never be able to keep from talking about the *very* fact that he *was* so brilliantly clever, as you put it. So he'd give himself away just the same.

Brandon Yes. But he *might* be so clever.

Rupert Might. But wouldn't.

There is a slight pause

(*Looking at Brandon*) Don't you think so?

There is a roll of thunder in the distance

Raglan Ah — here we are. It's coming back again.

Brandon (*going over to the window*) Lord, yes. I'm getting sick of this storm.

Leila Yes. So am I. I say, you know, it's really about time I ought to be going.

Raglan Yes. Same here, really.

Rupert (*drily*) What an uncanny coincidence. Now you'll both be able to go together.

There is another, louder, clap of thunder

Leila I say — isn't it *absolutely* awful?

Raglan Isn't it terrible? (*To Brandon*) Are you really still going, you two?

Brandon Certainly. It's probably only just around London. Besides — it's not so bad now. It's not raining, as a matter of fact, now, if you're thinking of getting off.

Leila No — that's what I thought.

Raglan Same here.

Rupert Which is another curious coincidence.

Leila Oh, do shut up — —

The telephone rings

Brandon Ah-ha ... (*He goes over to the telephone and sits down at it*)

The others listen to the following in complete silence

> (*Into the telephone*) Hallo. ... Hallohallohallo. ... Yes. ... Mayfair X142.
> ... Hallo. ... Yes. ...

There is a clap of thunder

> Hallo. ... Sorry — I can't hear. It's thundering this end. ... What? ... Who?
> ... Who? ... Oh! ... Yes. Yes, rather. Will you hold the line a minute and
> I'll get him. Right you are. Just hold on. (*He rises*) Sir Johnstone ...

Brandon exits

*There is a silence. Raglan grins at Leila. She grins back, then moves down
to the fireplace and looks into the fire. Rupert rises very abruptly. He hobbles
over to the sideboard and pours himself out a stiff drink. He gulps at it, takes
some more, and gulps again. He seems, for the first time, rather nervous. He
sits on the chest*

*The voices of Sir Johnstone and Brandon are heard coming from the other
room, then along the passage*

> *Sir Johnstone and Brandon enter. Sir Johnstone has obviously had a very
> satisfactory time with the books. He leaves off talking and goes cheerfully
> over to the telephone and takes up the receiver*

The others are perfectly still during the following

Sir Johnstone Hallo — hallo — hallo. ... Hallo, hallo ... (*To the others*) No-
one here ... Oh, hallo — yes? ... Oh yes. That you, dear? Oh, yes? ... Ye-
e-e-es. ... Ye-e-e-es. ... No, no. ... He's not here. ... Yes, yes, that's right.

> *Granillo and Mrs Debenham enter. Granillo is talking, but immediately
> senses the silence of the others, and becomes as quiet as them*

*Sir Johnstone turns round and looks at them for a moment as he listens on
the telephone, and then turns back again*

> Yes, yes. That's quite correct. ... Quite right, dear ... What? Oh, no, no.
> He'll be back soon, I expect. Probably held up in the — What? ... Oh yes,
> dear. ... Well — I'll be back there soon now. I'll be coming pretty well
> straight away. ... What? ... Yes. ... Right you are. Right you are. ...
> Goodbye. (*He puts the receiver down. He looks thoughtful and suddenly
> a trifle older and more lonely. Pause*) Ronald hasn't come back ...

Rupert Hasn't come back?

Sir Johnstone (*looking first at Rupert and then in front of him*) No …

Granillo Oh, that's the storm.

Sir Johnstone Yes. That's what it must be.

Rupert (*acidly*) Didn't you say he'd been to the Coliseum?

Sir Johnstone That's right.

Rupert I am disliking the telephone tonight.

Brandon Was he expected back, then, sir?

Sir Johnstone Yes. Apparently he arranged to get back to tea. My wife gets so alarmed if there's any hitch.

Brandon He'll probably be back by the time you get home.

Sir Johnstone Yes … yes, I expect he will. (*Brightening*) Well, we must be off. Where did we leave our hats and coats? Oh — downstairs.

Brandon Yes. I'll go and get them.

Brandon exits

Granillo pours himself another drink

Leila (*to Sir Johnstone*) Well — we've got your parcel all ready. (*She shows the parcel to him*)

Sir Johnstone Oh — that *is* sweet of you. Thank you very much. That's a wonderful parcel, isn't it?

Leila Well, it's not bad, is it?

Sir Johnstone I should say not. Yes … (*He becomes rather listless*) That's very convenient …

Brandon enters with Sir Johnstone's hat and coat

Brandon Here you are, Sir Johnstone. And it's not raining now.

Brandon helps Sir Johnstone on with his coat

But I do expect you'd like a taxi, wouldn't you?

Sir Johnstone Yes. I think I'd like a taxi. I'd rather like to get back. I can't think where that boy's got to … Thank you. I've never known him fail when he's said he'd be back.

Brandon Then he must be very filial, sir.

Sir Johnstone Yes. He is. Well, then, it only remains to thank you for the most charming evening, to say nothing of the most charming company, the company being even more delightful than the books, and that's saying an enormous amount. (*He smiles*) Well. (*To Leila*) Good-night — —

Leila Good-night.

Sir Johnstone (*to Raglan*) Good-night.

Raglan Good-night, sir.
Sir Johnstone Good-night, Mr Cadell.
Rupert Good-night, sir. (*During the following he moves to the window and looks out*)

Granillo pours another drink

Sir Johnstone looks at Granillo

Sir Johnstone (*moving towards the door*) And I'll have to give you something in exchange for those books, you know.
Brandon Never, sir.
Sir Johnstone Oh, yes. You must have something back. You must have some swaps, as we used to say. You must have your swaps. Oh, yes ...
Brandon No, you're forgetting them, sir.

Leila brings the books to Sir Johnstone and puts them shyly and kindly into his hand

Sir Johnstone Ah — thank you. That won't do, will it? Just like me. Just like me. I'm getting on, you know. I'm getting old, that's my trouble.

Sir Johnstone exits in a rather bewildered way, followed by Brandon

Mrs Debenham smiles a farewell all round. The others all murmur "Good-night" and smile

Mrs Debenham exits. Granillo follows her out

Leila (*yawning*) Oh dear. Well — I'm going too.
Raglan What part do you have to go to?
Leila Oh — I'm South Kensingtonish.
Raglan Oh, then we'll get a taxi, shall we? And I'll drop you.
Rupert (*moving* DS) Where, then, do *you* live, Mr Raglan?
Raglan Me? Oh — I live up at Hampstead.
Rupert Oh, I see. Then it'll be quite easy to drop her.
Leila I wish you'd drop your sarcastic remarks.
Rupert Pardon, pardon. I crave your pardon. I'm always suspecting "Love's Young (*he gives a ferocious blow with his stick on his chest as he brings out the next word*) Dream" when it's non-existent.

Brandon and Granillo enter. Granillo is still staggering slightly

Brandon Well, well.

Leila Well — I suppose we must go now.
Brandon Oh — won't you stay and have another spot?
Leila Oh, no. I don't think so. Thanks awfully. I think I ought to be going.
Raglan Yes. Same here, really.
Rupert Yes. I thought so.
Leila (*to Brandon, looking at Granillo reproachfully*) Well, if you're still going tonight, I certainly wouldn't let *him* drive.
Granillo Whadyoumean?
Brandon I will not, Leila. You may be sure. You ought to be ashamed of yourself, Granno.
Leila He certainly ought.
Granillo Whadyoumean? (*He tries to grin. He moves to the sideboard and pours a drink during the following*)

Raglan looks nervous and shy

Leila (*departingly*) Well … ?
Brandon Well … ?
Raglan Well … ?

Leila, Brandon and Raglan exit

Rupert follows them to the door but stops there

Rupert Good-night, Granillo.
Granillo (*turning round, as though startled*) Good-night, Rupert.

Rupert exits

Granillo sips at his drink and looks in front of him blankly and miserably. He staggers DS to a chair and bangs his glass down on the table. He puts his head in his hands

Brandon enters. He stops for a moment in the doorway with a little smile of satisfaction on his lips. He goes over to the window and draws the curtains to, then moves to the sideboard and pours himself out a drink

Brandon Well?
Granillo (*from behind his hands*) Well?
Brandon (*picking up his his drink with relish*) All's well. (*He moves down to the chest and plants his foot on it*)
Granillo God! I thought he got on to it.
Brandon Who? Rupert?
Granillo Yes.

Brandon Yes. So did I. For a few moments. But that's what gave piquancy
to the evening. He hadn't.

Granillo You're sure he hadn't?

Brandon Quite sure. (*He drinks. Pause*) I sometimes rather wish he had.
God. Rupert. Queer lad. I wonder. (*Reflectively*) If he had been with us he
wouldn't have got drunk, Granno.

Granillo (*looking up from his hands*) I not drunk — I'm a little blurred, that's
all. (*He sits up stiffly*) Hallo! What's that?

Brandon What?

Granillo I thought I heard something.

Brandon Be yourself, Granno.

Granillo I thought it was the bell.

There is a pause. Both listen

The bell is heard ringing

It was! It was!

Brandon (*sipping his drink; evenly*) Well. (*He gulps*) What of it? (*He
carefully finishes his drink*) I'll go down.

Brandon puts down his glass and exits

There is a long pause. Granillo looks in front of him steadily

The voices of Brandon and Rupert are heard from downstairs

Brandon enters suddenly, obviously having run up the stairs

Brandon (*moving to the mantelpiece, rather flustered*) It's Rupert. He's left
his cigarette case behind, apparently. Have you seen it?

Granillo No.

Brandon (*looking at one table, then at the chest, then at the second table*)
Well, it must be here somewhere.

*Rupert appears in the doorway. He has his overcoat on, and his hat in his
hand*

*For a moment neither Brandon nor Granillo sees Rupert. Then Brandon sees
him*

Brandon Hallo. You came up?

Rupert Yes … (*He slowly takes off his coat, and places it, with his hat, on the divan. He moves* DS)

Brandon and Granillo watch Rupert intently

I thought you might give me another spot. (*He sits down*)

CURTAIN

ACT III

The scene is the same as before, and no time has elapsed

Brandon You're welcome, Rupert. (*He moves to the sideboard and pours Rupert a whisky*)

Rupert (*calmly producing his cigarette case from his hip pocket and holding it up*) I beg your pardon. Humbly.

Brandon (*from the sideboard*) Why? (*He sees the cigarette case*) Oh! You ass! (*He indicates the soda syphon*) Just a splash, Rupert?

Rupert Yes. A generous one.

Brandon squirts soda water into the glass then takes it over to Rupert

Rupert takes a cigarette from the case and lights it. He takes the whisky from Brandon

Brandon sits on the chest

Oh, dear heaven! What unmentionable fatigue.

Brandon What?

Rupert Living, living, living. I wonder if this is a way out. (*He looks at his glass*) I shall try Omarism one day.

> "The mighty Mahmud, the victorious lord,
> Whom all the misbelieving and black horde
> Of fears and horrors (*rather stressed*) that infest the soul,
> Scatters and slays with this enchanted sword."

Granno seems to agree with that.

Brandon Yes. But he's not going to get any more.

Rupert You're in a horrible state tonight, Granillo. You're positively silent drunk.

Granillo (*rising and going over to the mantelpiece for a cigarette*) Oh — I'm all right. (*He lights the cigarette and returns to his seat, walking quite fairly steadily*)

Rupert I say. Must we have all this light?

Granillo What's wrong with the light?

Rupert Nothing is *wrong* with the light, Granillo. Only I am a creature of half-lights, and seeing that you have a very pleasantly shaded little table lamp, can't we make use of it?

Brandon (*rising and moving to the lamp*) Yes. I quite agree. (*He switches the lamp on and moves to the light switch by the door*) But I hope you're not going to settle down *too* heavily, and make yourself *too* much at home, because we've got to be off before long. (*He switches the overhead lights off*)

The room is lit by the table lamp only

Rupert Ah — that's better. (*Crossing his legs and leaning back*) Much better. I am sad tonight, you know. What's the time?
Brandon (*looking at the clock*) About five-and-twenty to eleven.
Rupert Five-and-twenty to eleven. I expect you're wanting to get rid of me, aren't you?
Brandon Not at all, Rupert.
Rupert I hope not. I'm full of melancholy, and don't want to go home ... You must bear with me ... It's been such a strange evening ...
Brandon Strange evening — why?
Granillo (*quickly*) Why strange?
Rupert I can't tell you. That's my trouble. I suppose it's the thunder, and one thing and another. (*He drinks*) Thunder always upsets me. Besides, I'm always melancholy at this hour. Five-and-twenty to eleven. It's a curious hour ... Did you ever read Goldsmith's *Nightpiece*?
Brandon No. I can't actually recall it.
Rupert No? You should. It's about the city at night. I shall do his *Nightpiece* up to date one of these days. And I shall make it five-and-twenty to eleven. Now. It's a wonderful hour. I am particularly susceptible to it.
Brandon Why so wonderful?
Rupert Because it is, I think, the hour when London asks why — when it wants to know what it's all about — when the tedium of activity and the folly of pleasure are equally transparent. It is the hour in which unemployed servant girls, and the spoiled beauties of slums, walk the streets for hire ... It is the hour of winking advertisement signs, and taxis, and buses, and traffic blocks. It is the hour when jaded London theatre audiences are settling down in the darkness to the last acts of plays, of which they know the denouement only too well. They know that when the curtain's down, it'll be just a question of "God Save the King", and they'll be bundled out into a chilly and possibly rainy night, where they'll have to fight for taxis, or rush for trains, or somehow transport themselves home to a cold supper and the prospect of another day tomorrow exactly similar to that which has passed. For others, further horrors are awaiting. The nightclubs and cabarets have not yet begun, but they will do so very soon ... I could enlarge upon the idea indefinitely. Five-and-twenty to eleven. A horrible hour — a *macabre* hour, for it is not only the hour of pleasure ended, it is the hour

when pleasure itself has been found wanting. There, that is what this hour means to me, and it has, moreover, been thundery. Five-and-twenty to eleven ...

Brandon Yes, Rupert, but by the time you have finished making your speech it will be eleven o' clock. In brief, my dear Rupert, you see no earthly object in living?

Rupert I fear not. Do you?

Brandon I? Yes. Of course I do. But then I'm interested in things. Why don't you get interested in things? Why don't you take up exploring, or cricket, or making love, or golf, or finance, or lecturing, or something?

Rupert Or, as you suggested this evening, murder.

Pause

Brandon Or, as you say, murder. (*He finishes his drink and switches the overhead light on*) Now, Rupert. We don't want to turn you *out* ...

Rupert Oh, surely you're not going to do that? Surely you're not going to spoil my mood?

Brandon No. We're not going to spoil any of your moods, but we've got to get going some time. And we've got a bit of packing to do and one thing and another.

Rupert Oh, you really mustn't spoil my mood. I shall write something tonight if I go on like this. You can't be so cruel. Can't I have another drink?

Brandon (*coming down to Rupert for his glass and taking it back to the sideboard again*) Certainly, Rupert. There's no hurry whatever. Only a poetic frame of mind will hardly be induced by the spectacle of Granno and me filling suitcases.

Rupert Oh, I certainly think it would. Can't I stay and watch you?

Brandon (*giving Rupert his drink*) Well — we'll see. You know, I believe *you're* a bit blotto tonight too, Rupert.

Rupert I wouldn't be surprised. (*He drinks*) I'll tell you what — I'll stay and see you off.

Granillo rises suddenly and pours himself out another enormous drink. Brandon goes over to him

Brandon That's enough of that, Granno.

Granillo Mind your own business.

Brandon Come along, Granno. That's enough.

Granillo (*banging his glass on the sideboard; louder*) Mind your own business! (*He moves* DS)

Brandon (*coming* DC *again*) Well, it's not my business. (*Brightly*) Stay and see us off, Rupert? All right. You finish that and see what you feel about it. Doesn't look as though we'll *get* off with Granno in this state.

Granillo I'm perf'ly sober. Why does he want to stay'n see us off? That's what I want to know. Why does he want to stay'n see us off?

Brandon My dear Granno. Rupert has no earthly reason in wanting to stay and see us off, and I don't know what you're talking about. There's no doing anything with you. I'm getting sick of this. Come along, Rupert, finish that up and leave him with me.

There is a pause during which Rupert looks at Brandon

Rupert Oh. I've got to go, then?

There is a long pause in which Brandon and Granillo both look at Rupert

Brandon (*very quietly and securely*) What do you mean, Rupert? You've "got to go"?

Rupert Oh. Nothing. I thought for a moment that perhaps *you* wanted me to go as well.

Brandon Nothing of the sort. I was getting fed up with all this silly chatter, and wanted to be alone with Granno, that's all. *I* don't want you to go.

Rupert You don't?

Brandon No.

Rupert All right, then. I'll stay. Can I have another drink? (*He holds out his glass*)

Granillo I said so! I said so ...

Brandon (*putting on a grin*) You're in a queer mood tonight, Rupert, too. (*He takes Brandon's glass to the sideboard*)

Rupert No — not a queer mood. An inspired mood, rather. One has inspirations, you know. Extraordinary inspirations. And I have one tonight.

Brandon Oh — what's that?

Rupert Ah — I'll tell you that, perhaps.

Granillo rises and goes towards the window. Rupert rises and stops him on the way

You haven't such a thing as a pin, Granillo, have you?

Granillo A what?

Rupert A pin.

Granillo (*feeling in his lapel*) Yes. (*He gives Rupert the pin*)

Rupert Thank you. (*He puts the pin straight into his own lapel*)

Granillo moves to the window

Brandon brings Rupert's drink to him

Ah — thank you. (*He takes a sip*) I shan't be long now.

Brandon No hurry. (*He looks at the clock, and then goes to the cupboard in the sideboard, and puts bottles and things away during the following*) It's past a quarter to, though. (*He yawns*) Oh Lord, I don't feel like driving tonight after all.

Rupert No — there's something in the air tonight. (*He takes the Coliseum ticket from his waistcoat pocket, and very calmly pins it on the outside of his lapel*) Did you notice Sir Johnstone's exit? (*He touches the ticket as though it were a flower*)

Brandon (*putting bottles away; casually*) No — what about it?

Rupert Rather subdued, I thought. (*He finishes off his drink*) And pathetic. Well, well, I must be going.

Rupert rises. Granillo is at the window, Brandon at the cupboard; neither sees Rupert. He hesitates, and then slowly hobbles to Granillo at the window. He opens the window and leans out

Rupert What's it doing?
Granillo S'better now.

Rupert remains at the window, looking out. Granillo moves down to the chest. He looks at Brandon, who looks at him. They exchange a satisfied glance. Granillo sits on the chest, hands in pockets, reeling a little

Rupert suddenly shuts the window, turns round, leans against the sill, and looks at Brandon and Granillo. They still do not observe him. Then he hobbles DS, and, putting his stick on his chest, he leans his face on his hands thoughtfully

Rupert Ah, well. And so to bed.
Brandon (*putting the last bottle away, and moving a little towards Rupert*) Well, Rupert — thank you very much for coming round and all that ...
Rupert (*in the same position, nodding his head*) The pleasure is mine. Mine altogether. Believe me. (*He brings his stick down and stands properly*)

Granillo rises, sobered completely, and stares at Rupert with horror

It's been a very interesting evening.
Brandon Hallo — what's your button-hole?

Rupert looks first at Brandon, and then at Granillo. He stays perfectly still, watching Granillo

Granillo (*slowly and tensely*) He's got it. (*Nodding*) He's got it.

Brandon Hold your tongue, Granno.

Granillo (*hysterically, not listening to Brandon*) Oh yes. He's got it all right. *Ah-ah-ah-ah!* (*He gives a terrible, piercing, falsetto scream, and bangs on his chest as he says the following*)

Granillo }(*together*) {He's got it! He's got it! He's got it!
Brandon }   {(*shaking Granillo; shouting even louder*) Hold your tongue! Hold your tongue! Hold your filthy tongue!

Rupert hobbles DR

Granillo (*groaning and staggering against the chest.*) Oh – oh – oh. (*He gives a low, long drawn-out, shuddering sob; during the following he sinks down beside the chest, still sobbing and breathing hard*)

Brandon (*with restrained violence*) Hold your row! Hold your row! (*He moves in the direction of Rupert and stops*) Rupert.

Rupert Yes.

Brandon Rupert. This is nothing to do with you. Granno and I have a certain trouble between us which concerns no-one else. Will you kindly oblige us by going at once and leaving us to it?

Rupert (*looking down at his stick*) Won't you tell me your trouble, Brandon? I might be able to help.

Brandon No. I will not tell you our trouble. (*He moves towards the door*) Please go. It's nothing to do with you.

Rupert (*still looking down at his stick*) No, Brandon, it may not be anything to do with me. But it may possibly be something to do with — with the public in general — and I'm its only representative in this room. Won't you tell me?

Brandon comes forward menacingly, and, to his surprise, Rupert comes forward to meet him

Brandon Are you going, or are you not?

They glare into each other's eyes. There is a slow moan from Granillo. Pause

Rupert No, Brandon, I'm not going. You see, I'm rather awkwardly situated …

Brandon (*more menacingly still; a change in his tone*) You are something more than that, my friend.

Rupert (*holding his ground; a trifle breathlessly*) Oh — how's that?

Brandon You are very dangerously situated. (*He suddenly moves forward*)

Rupert retreats, putting up his stick to protect himself. Brandon seizes it without the slightest difficulty, and brings it down to a horizontal level. They each hold firmly to the stick and gaze at the other

Very dangerously situated, indeed.

Rupert (*after a pause*) Brandon. I am lame, and I have no protection.

Brandon You have not.

Rupert Save that of my foresight.

Brandon Your foresight?

*Rupert pulls on the handle of the stick and withdraws a blade from it —
revealing it as a swordstick. There is a flash of steel. Brandon is left with the
empty wooden sheath in his hand*

Rupert But this is a compensation as well as an encumbrance. (*He hobbles
sideways* US *quickly, with the sword between him and the others*) Besides,
I have another little weapon, which is of even greater value to me. (*He
produces a little silver whistle*)

Brandon What's that?

Rupert This? (*He holds it up*) A whistle. A policeman gave it to me.

*Brandon walks rapidly over to Rupert. Rupert puts himself in a defensive
position. Brandon pauses, and then goes over to pour himself out a drink*

Brandon (*quite calmly*) Oh! And when did he give you that?

Rupert He gave it to me twenty minutes ago. Before I came back — for my
cigarette case. He is now waiting for me to use it. He is waiting at the corner.
It depends upon you whether I shall use it or not.

Brandon What do you want from me, Rupert?

Rupert I want two things — two truths. I want the truth about this ticket here
(*he tears it off his jacket*) and the truth about that chest there — or rather
its contents.

Brandon I can satisfy you on both. As for the ticket, I know nothing whatever
about it. As for the chest, I simply do not know what you mean.

Rupert You have succeeded in satisfying me on neither.

Brandon (*moving a little towards Rupert*) Rupert, I have come to the
conclusion that you are hopelessly drunk, and that you had better go home.

Rupert It is possible that I am drunk — but not hopelessly. And I am not
going home.

Brandon What is all this about? What is all this maudlin suspiciousness?

Rupert This is not maudlin suspiciousness, Brandon. It is well-founded.
From the first moment, when I telephoned this house at a quarter to nine,
and heard, over the wire, your friend there (*pointing to Granillo*) crying for
the dark, suspicion was there. And that suspicion has been growing ever
since.

Brandon Growing ever since! Growing ever since! What do you mean?
What do you suspect?

Rupert I suspect murder, Brandon. The murder of Ronald Kentley.

Brandon Rupert. Have you gone mad?

Rupert I dare say so. Perhaps you will prove that I have.

Brandon You suspect *what*, did you say?

Rupert Murder, Brandon.

Brandon (*feigning relief*) Oh, my God! My poor, poor Rupert! You don't know how you've relieved me. I imagined you'd got on to the real truth, which'd have been devilish awkward. Murder! Oh dear, that's good. (*To Granillo on the ground*) Hear that, Granno. He suspects us of murder! Murder! Isn't that too rich?

Rupert Is it possible that you are trying to bluff me?

Brandon Bluff you — you drunken sot and maniac! Bluff you! Get on out of here! Blow your whistle, and bring your policeman in! Get on out! Do what you like!

Rupert Ah — perhaps I am insane, then. But since you say I can do what I like, may I see the inside of that chest?

Brandon See the inside of that chest! See the inside of that chest! You can see the inside of fifty thousand chests! Get on out!

Rupert (*very calmly*) I did not ask to see the inside of fifty thousand chests, Brandon, but to see the inside of that specific chest. And I cannot do that if I have to "get on out".

Brandon You're mad and drunk!

Rupert Possibly. Nevertheless, may I look inside that chest?

Brandon (*shouting*) Yes!

There is a tremendous and baffling silence. Rupert hobbles DL, and pauses to look at Brandon in a puzzled way, then hobbles towards the window and looks at him again in the same way. He moves DC. Pause

Rupert Very well. I will.

There is another pause as they look at each other. Brandon moves fairly near to the chest

Brandon Go on. What are you waiting for?

Rupert You're very clever, Brandon, in any case.

Brandon I wish I could say the same of you, you fantastic ass. (*He advances a little on Rupert*)

Rupert Will you get farthest away, please? Will you go down to that chair? (*He points with the sword to the chair R*)

Brandon obeys. Rupert pauses, then goes to the chest. Granillo is still prostrate. Rupert examines the lock and tries to lift the lid

It's locked — padlocked. (*He sits easily on the edge of the chest*)

Brandon What of it?

Rupert Where's the key?

Brandon I don't know. Why should I know? It's upstairs, I think.

Rupert Upstairs?

Brandon Yes. Shall I go and get it?

Rupert (*rising*) No. Don't do that. (*He moves over to the sideboard and picks up the silver nutcrackers*) I can force it. (*He moves* DS *again, looking at the others*) Must I do this?

There is no answer from Brandon

Must I do this?

Brandon (*suddenly blazing*) Here's your key! Here's your key! (*He fishes the key out of his waistcoat pocket and flings it down*) Now look — and get what's coming to you!

Rupert Thank you.

Rupert picks up the key and begins to fumble with the lock. Brandon leaps forward, but Rupert is too quick for him. He swings round into a sitting posture on the chest, and has his sword pointed at the other's breast

Brandon You'll be sorry if you look in there, Cadell! You'll be sorry.

Rupert I'll take the risk. Will you go back to that chair?

Brandon obeys. Rupert goes on fumbling. He unlocks the chest. He pauses before opening the chest, and looks at Brandon. Then he slowly lifts the lid and looks in. There is a long pause. Suddenly the lid comes down with a smash. Rupert literally runs, in so far as his lameness will allow him, towards the door. The thing has obviously appalled him more than he could have imagined. He turns round and runs in the same way UC. *There he stops, completely overcome*

Oh — you swine ... (*He wipes his hand across his mouth, his lips at once contemptuous and horror-struck*) You dirty swine ... (*He gives a shuddering sob*)

Brandon (*quietly*) Now then, Rupert. Sit down. I want to talk to you.

Rupert Poor Ronald Kentley ... What had he done to you? (*He moves* DS *a little*)

Brandon Sit down, Rupert. For God's sake sit down. I want to talk to you.

Rupert (*pulling himself together*) Sit down, Brandon? What do you mean?

Brandon (*standing; louder*) Sit down! For God's sake sit down and listen. I want to explain!

Rupert Explain?

Brandon (*giving way slightly*) Oh, sit down. For God's sake sit down! I'm at your mercy, I tell you, I'm at your mercy. Have mercy on me! I can explain! Have mercy on me! Sit down and judge me! Sit down and judge me!

Rupert slowly comes and sits DL

Rupert Well?

Brandon paces up towards the window before sitting DC. *He thinks, putting his face in his hands*

Brandon Rupert. You're an enlightened man, aren't you?

Rupert I profess to be. Yes.

Brandon And it is in your power to have me — hanged.

Rupert So it seems.

Brandon And Granillo too.

Rupert And Granillo too.

Brandon Rupert.

Rupert Yes.

Brandon You remember our talk tonight — about the Old Bailey and justice?

Rupert Yes. Well.

Brandon And the difference between the two. You made the point.

Rupert Yes.

Brandon Yes. Well. Remember that. You wouldn't be giving us up to justice. And now I want to ask you something else. You are not a man of morals, are you?

Rupert No. I'm not.

Brandon And you do not rate life as a very precious thing, do you?

Rupert No.

Brandon Now listen, Rupert. Listen. I have done this thing. I and Granno. We have done it together. We have done it for — for adventure. For adventure and danger. For danger. You read Nietzsche, don't you, Rupert?

Rupert Yes.

Brandon And you know that he tells us to live dangerously.

Rupert Yes.

Brandon And you know that he's no more respect for individual life than you, and tells us — to — live dangerously. We thought we would do so — that's all. We have done so. We have only *done* the thing. Others have talked. We have done. Do you understand?

Rupert Go on.

Brandon Listen, Rupert, listen. You're understanding, I think. You're the
one man to understand. Now apart from all that — quite apart — even if
you can't see how we — look at it, you'll see that you can't give us up. Two
lives can't recall one. It'd just be triple murder. You would never allow that.
But apart from that too — our lives are in your hands. You can't kill us. You
can't kill. If you have us up now, it'd be killing us as much as if you were
to run us through with that sword in your hand. You're not a murderer,
Rupert.

Rupert What are you?

Brandon We aren't, we *aren't*, I tell you! Don't tell me you're a slave of your
period. In the days of Borgias you'd have thought nothing of this. For
God's sake tell me you're an emancipated man. Rupert, you can't give us
up. You know you can't. You can't. You can't! You can't ... (*A long pause*)
Can you?

Pause

Rupert Yes, I know. There's every truth in what you've said. This is a very
queer, dark and incomprehensible universe, and I understand it little. I
myself have always tried to apply pure logic to it, and the application of
logic can lead us into strange passes. It has done so in this case. You have
brought up my own words in my face, and a man should stand by his own
words. I shall never trust in logic again. You have said that I hold life cheap.
You're right. I do. Your own included. (*He rises*)

Brandon What do you mean?

Rupert (*suddenly letting himself go — a thing he has not done all the
evening, and which he now does with tremendous force, and clear, angry
articulation*) What do I mean? What do I mean? I mean that you have taken
and killed — by strangulation — a very harmless and helpless fellow-
creature of twenty years. I mean that in that chest there — now lie the
staring and futile remains of something that four hours ago lived, and
laughed, and ran, and found it good. Laughed as you could never laugh, and
ran as you could never run. I mean that, for your cruel and scheming
pleasure, you have committed a sin and blasphemy against that very life
which you now find yourselves so precious. And you have done more than
this. You have not only killed him; you have rotted the lives of all those to
whom he was dear. And you have brought worse than death to his father
— an equally harmless old man who has fought his way quietly through
to a peaceful end, and to whom the whole universe, after this, will now be
blackened and distorted beyond the limits of thought. That is what you
have done. And in dragging him round here tonight, you have played a
lewd and infamous jest upon him — and a bad jest at that. And if you think,

as your type of philosopher generally does, that all life is nothing but a bad jest, then you will now have the pleasure of seeing it played upon yourselves.

Brandon (*pale and frozen*) What are you saying? What are you doing?

Rupert It is not what *I* am doing, Brandon. It is what society is going to do. And what will happen to you at the hands of society I am not in a position to tell you. That's its own business. But I can give you a pretty shrewd guess, I think. (*He moves forward to the chest and swings back the lid*) You are going to hang, you swine! Hang! Both of you! *Hang!*(*Whistle in hand, he runs hobbling to the window, throws it open, leans out, and sends three piercing whistles into the night*)

CURTAIN

FURNITURE AND PROPERTY LIST

ACT I

On stage: *On mantelpiece*: books, box of cigarettes, matches
By fireplace: coal, fire irons
Grandfather clock set to eight-forty
Wireless set
Large divan
Two armchairs, DR and DL
By DL armchair: small table with ashtray on it
By DR armchair: small table with lamp and book on it
Baby grand piano
Sideboard with glasses, drinks (including wine, whisky and champagne)
 and pair of silver nutcrackers on it
Large chest
Telephone
Window curtains open

Off stage: Blue Coliseum ticket (**Brandon**)
Newspaper (**Sabot**)
Large tray of table linen, cutlery, plates, sandwiches (**Sabot**)

Personal: **Granillo**: wrist-watch, handkerchief
Rupert: swordstick, spectacles in case, handkerchief
Brandon: handkerchief

ACT II

Re-set: Hands of grandfather clock

Off stage: Books (**Raglan**)
Wrapping paper, cigarettes, ball of string (**Raglan**)

ACT III

Re-set: Hands of grandfather clock to ten-thirty-five

Personal: **Granillo**: pin
Rupert: whistle

LIGHTING PLOT

Practical fittings required: table lamp, fire effect in grate
One interior with exterior backings beyond doors and window. The same throughout

ACT I

To open: Pallid gleam from lamplight beyond window

Cue 1	**Brandon** switches on the lamp *Snap on practical lamp and covering spot*	(Page 2)
Cue 2	**Brandon** switches off the lamp *Snap off practical lamp and covering spot*	(Page 2)
Cue 3	**Granillo**: "No. You mayn't …" *Bring up faint fireglow from grate*	(Page 3)
Cue 4	**Brandon** switches on the lamp *Snap on practical lamp and covering spot*	(Page 5)
Cue 5	**Brandon** switches off the lamp *Snap off practical lamp and covering spot*	(Page 5)
Cue 6	**Granillo** shuts the door behind him. Click *Snap on light on backing beyond door; pause; snap off*	(Page 5)
Cue 7	**Granillo** lights a match and holds it up to the clock *Covering spot on match until it goes out*	(Page 6)
Cue 8	**Brandon** switches on the lamp *Snap on practical lamp and covering spot*	(Page 6)
Cue 9	**Brandon** switches on the overhead light *Snap on general interior lighting*	(Page 7)
Cue 10	**Brandon** exits, closing the door. Click *Snap on light on backing beyond door*	(Page 7)

ACT II

To open: General interior lighting including table lamp; pallid gleam from lamplight beyond window; light on backing beyond door

Cue 11	**Brandon** switches off the lamp and the overhead light *Snap off lamp and general interior lighting*	(Page 32)
Cue 12	Gramophone ceases. Pause *Snap off light on door backing; snap back on*	(Page 33)
Cue 13	**Brandon** switches on the lamp *Snap on practical lamp and covering spot*	(Page 33)
Cue 14	**Brandon** switches on the overhead lights *Snap on general interior lighting*	(Page 33)
Cue 15	**Brandon** switches off the lamp *Snap off practical lamp and covering spot*	(Page 33)

ACT III

To open: General interior lighting; pallid gleam from lamplight beyond window; light on backing beyond door

Cue 16	**Brandon** switches the lamp on *Snap on practical lamp*	(Page 55)
Cue 17	**Brandon** switches off the overhead light *Snap off general interior lighting*	(Page 55)
Cue 18	**Brandon** switches on the overhead light *Snap on general interior lighting*	(Page 55)

EFFECTS PLOT

ACT I

Cue 1   **Brandon**: "The same thing applies to her."   (Page 5)
Telephone

Cue 2   **Granillo** creeps out into the passage and closes the door   (Page 5)
Click

Cue 3   **Brandon** exits, closing the door   (Page 7)
Click

Cue 4   **Brandon**: " … it got there I don't know."   (Page 7)
Doorbell

Cue 5   **Brandon**: "Also of Jim and Amy ..."   (Page 9)
Doorbell

Cue 6   **Granillo**: "I'm very harmless."   (Page 12)
Doorbell

Cue 7   **Leila**: "Such a queer time, to begin with."   (Page 14)
Doorbell

Cue 8   **Brandon**: " … I'm told it's very fine."   (Page 16)
Doorbell

Cue 9   **Rupert**: "Ah, that's what *I* do …"   (Page 25)
Gramophone from offstage

Cue 10   **Rupert**: "Listen."   (Page 25)
Bring up sound of rain. Cut gramophone

Cue 11   **Rupert** turns the pages of the book   (Page 26)
*Gramophone from off stage; suddenly increase volume
     as if door has opened, then fade gradually*

Cue 12   **Sabot**: "Very well, thank you, sair." Pause   (Page 26)
Increase volume of rain sound

Cue 13   **Brandon** stands up and looks at **Rupert**   (Page 30)
Snap on gramophone off stage

ACT II

Cue 14	When ready	(Page 32)
	Bring up offstage gramophone as at the end of Act I; fade gradually. Rain sound continuously under scene	

Cue 15	**Rupert**: "Yes."	(Page 32)
	Gramophone from off stage	

Cue 16	**Brandon** draws the curtains back	(Page 33)
	Increase volume of rain sound; rain effect on window	

Cue 17	**Brandon** bends down to the lock	(Page 33)
	Gramophone ceases	

Cue 18	**Rupert**: " ... sure he's lifting all your best."	(Page 38)
	Sudden tremendous clap of thunder	

Cue 19	**Rupert**: "Hallo — here we are ..."	(Page 38)
	Clap of thunder, dying into the distance	

Cue 20	**Rupert**: "I thought it was coming,"	(Page 38)
	Enormous downpour of rain	

Cue 21	**Rupert**: "Surely — —"	(Page 38)
	Even more tremendous clap of thunder	

Cue 22	**Brandon**: "It'll clear up soon."	(Page 38)
	Clap of thunder	

Cue 23	**Brandon**: "It's this whisky."	(Page 41)
	Growl of thunder	

Cue 24	**Rupert**: "Don't you think so?"	(Page 47)
	Roll of thunder in the distance	

Cue 25	**Rupert**: "Now you'll both be able to go together."	(Page 47)
	Another, louder clap of thunder	

Cue 26	**Leila**: "Oh, do shut up — —"	(Page 47)
	Telephone rings	

Cue 27	**Brandon**: "Mayfair X142. ... Hallo. ... Yes. ..."	(Page 48)
	Clap of thunder	

Cue 28	**Granillo**: "I thought it was the bell." Pause	(Page 52)
	Doorbell	

ACT III

No cues